HOW TO DRAW VEHICLES

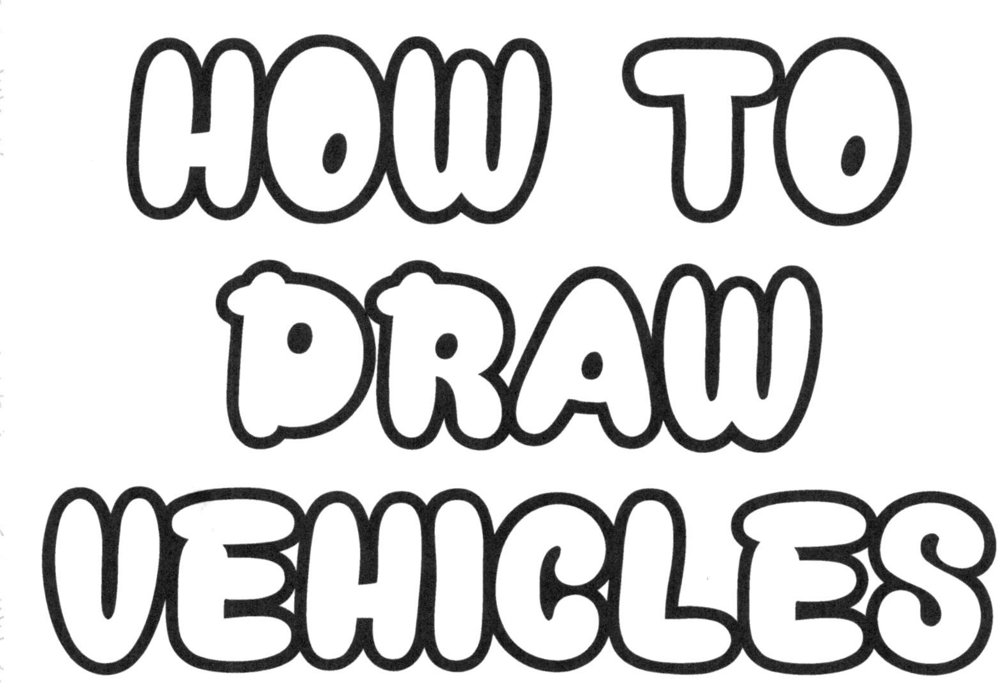

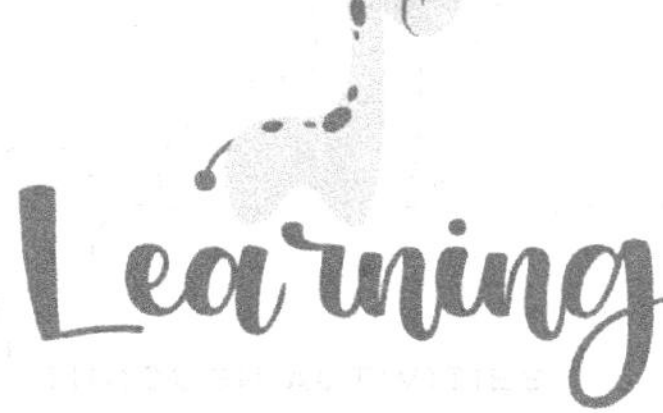

Learning

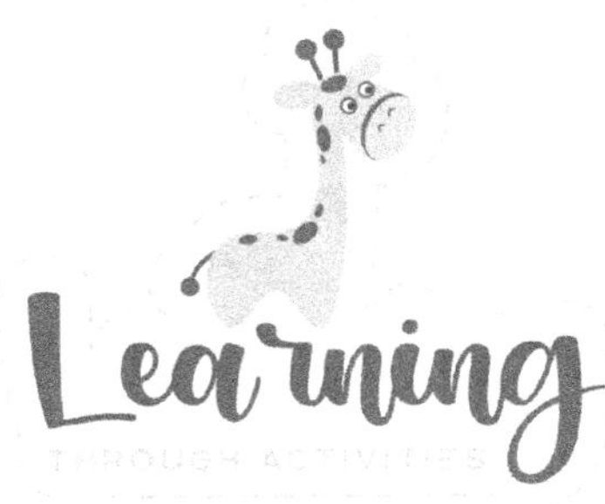

SPECIAL BONUS!

Want These 2 Books For FREE?

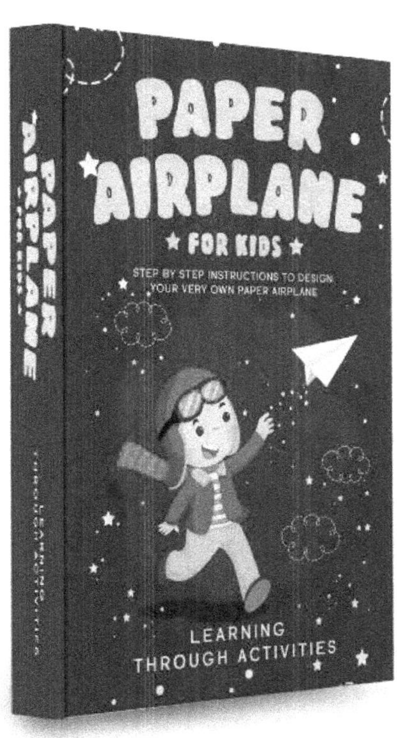

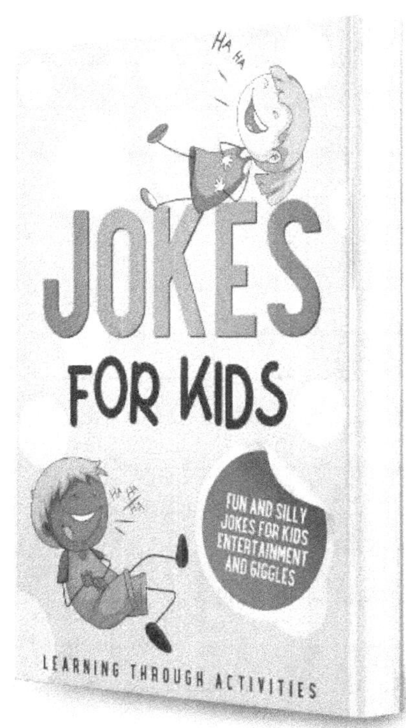

Get **FREE**, unlimited access to these and all of our new kids books by joining our community!

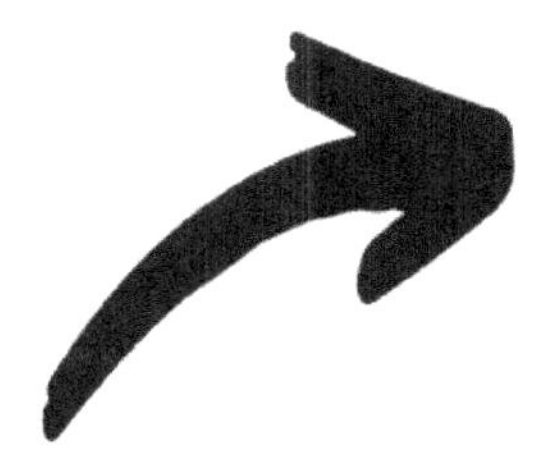

Scan W/ Your Camera To Join!

CONTENTS

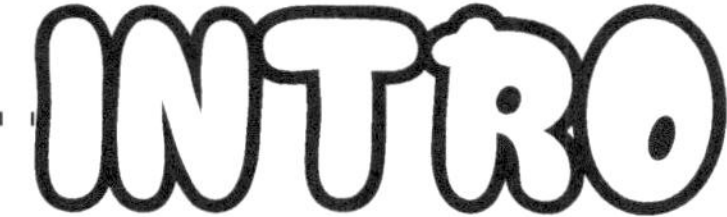

INTRO

WELCOME TO 'HOW TO DRAW VEHICLES.' THIS BOOK IS FULL OF ALL DIFFERENT KINDS OF THINGS THAT GO! YOU'LL BE AN ARTIST BEFORE YOU KNOW IT!

EACH VEHICLE HAS EASY TO FOLLOW INSTRUCTIONS THAT WILL STEP-BY-STEP HAVE YOU DRAWING THEM LIKE A PRO!

NOT ONLY WILL YOU LEARN HOW TO DRAW ALL OF THESE VEHICLES, YOU WILL ALSO LEARN THE MAIN USE OF THE VEHICLE, WHERE IT WAS FIRST MADE AND A FACT ABOUT EACH VEHICLE.

PLEASE DON'T WORRY IF YOUR VEHICLES TURN OUT A LITTLE DIFFERENT FROM THE ONES IN THE PICTURES, WE ALL HAVE OUR UNIQUE STYLE, AND ALSO, PRACTICE MAKES PERFECT!

GENERALLY, IT'S BEST TO START WITH A PENCIL WHILE YOU ARE GETTING THE HANG OF IT, SO LITTLE MISTAKES CAN BE EASILY ERASED. THEN MOVE ONTO PENS, COLORED, SPARKLY, WHATEVER YOU LIKE.

HAVE FUN!

BOAT

MAIN USE OF VEHICLE:
TO FLOAT ON WATER - TO TRANSPORT PEOPLE, GOODS, AND MORE.

WHERE IT WAS FIRST MADE:
THE ANCIENT EGYPTIANS WERE THE MOST LIKELY FIRST BOAT BUILDERS.

FACT ABOUT VEHICLE:
LAURA DEKKER, A 16-YEAR-OLD DUTCH SAILOR IS THE YOUNGEST PERSON TO SAIL AROUND THE WORLD ALONE.

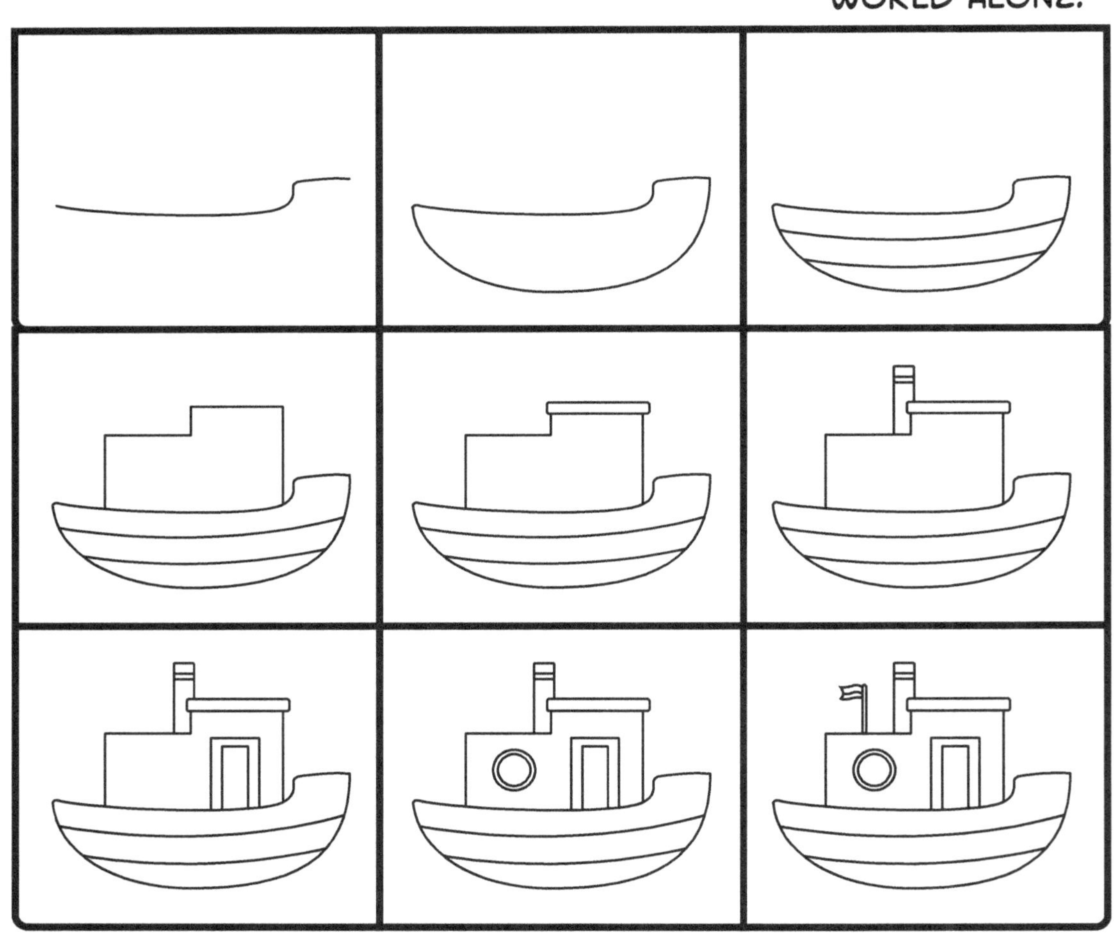

TRUCK

TO TRANSPORT GOODS FROM ONE POINT TO ANOTHER.

IN GERMANY IN 1896.

IF YOU LINED UP ALL THE TRUCKS IN THE US, THEY WOULD REACH THE MOON!

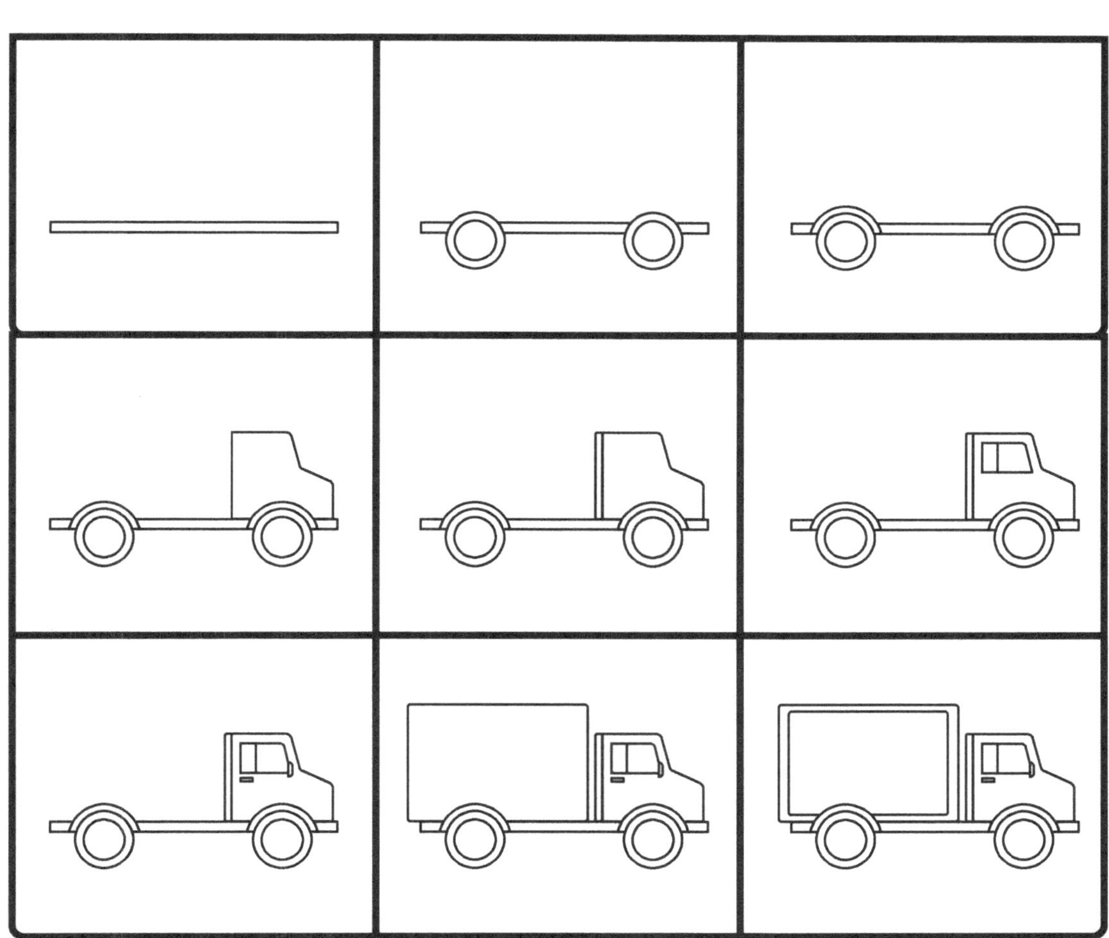

MOTORBIKE

GETTING ABOUT.

GERMANY IN 1885.

THE LONGEST MOTOR-CYCLE JUMP EVER WAS BY ROBBIE MADDISON IN MELBOURNE, AUSTRALIA, WHO JUMPED 107 M TO SET THE WORLD RE-CORD.

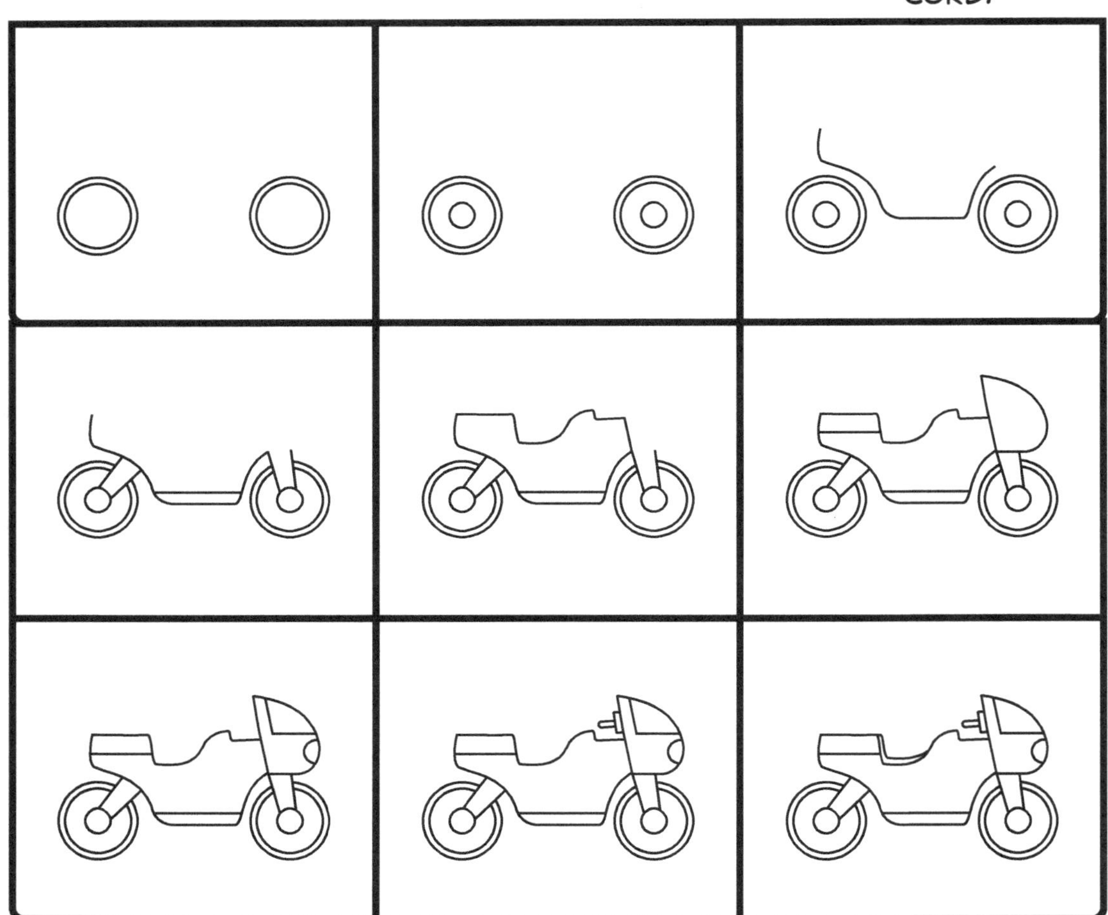

MAIN USE OF VEHICLE:

A WEAPON USED IN BATTLE.

WHERE IT WAS FIRST MADE:

ENGLAND 1915.

FACT ABOUT VEHICLE:

JACQUES LITTLEFIED, FROM SILICON VALLEY HAS COLLECTED AROUND 240 TANKS!

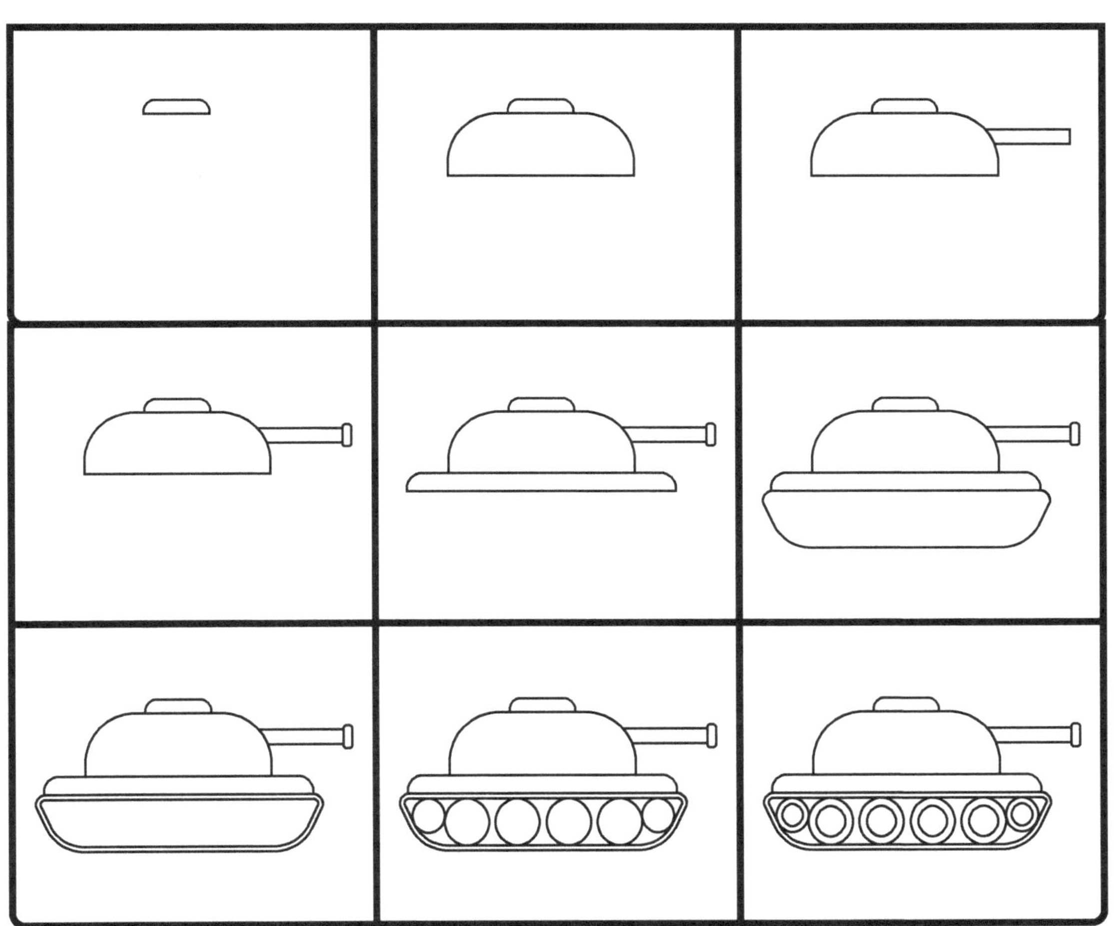

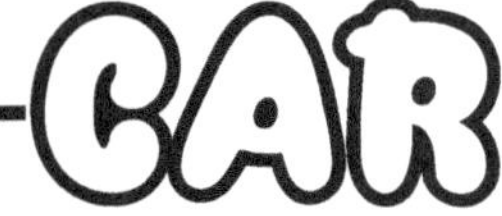CAR

MAIN USE OF VEHICLE:
TO MOVE PEOPLE ABOUT.

WHERE IT WAS FIRST MADE:
GERMANY 1888.

FACT ABOUT VEHICLE:
THE AVERAGE CAR IS MADE UP OF 30,000 PARTS.

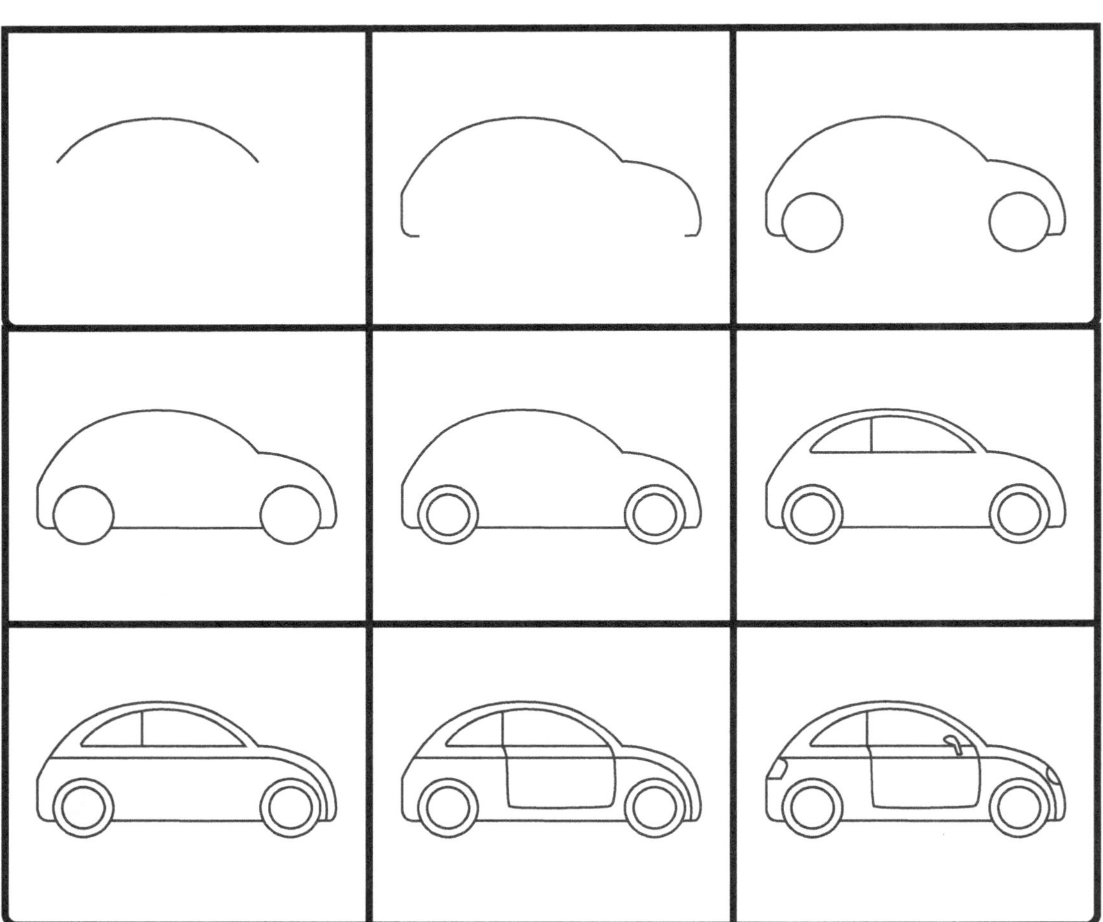

PLANE

MAIN USE OF VEHICLE:

TO MOVE PEOPLE AND CARGO OVER GREAT DISTANCES IN A SHORT AMOUNT OF TIME.

WHERE IT WAS FIRST MADE:

AMERICA 1903

FACT ABOUT VEHICLE:

AMELIA EARHART WAS THE FIRST WOMAN TO FLY BY HERSELF ACROSS THE ATLANTIC OCEAN.

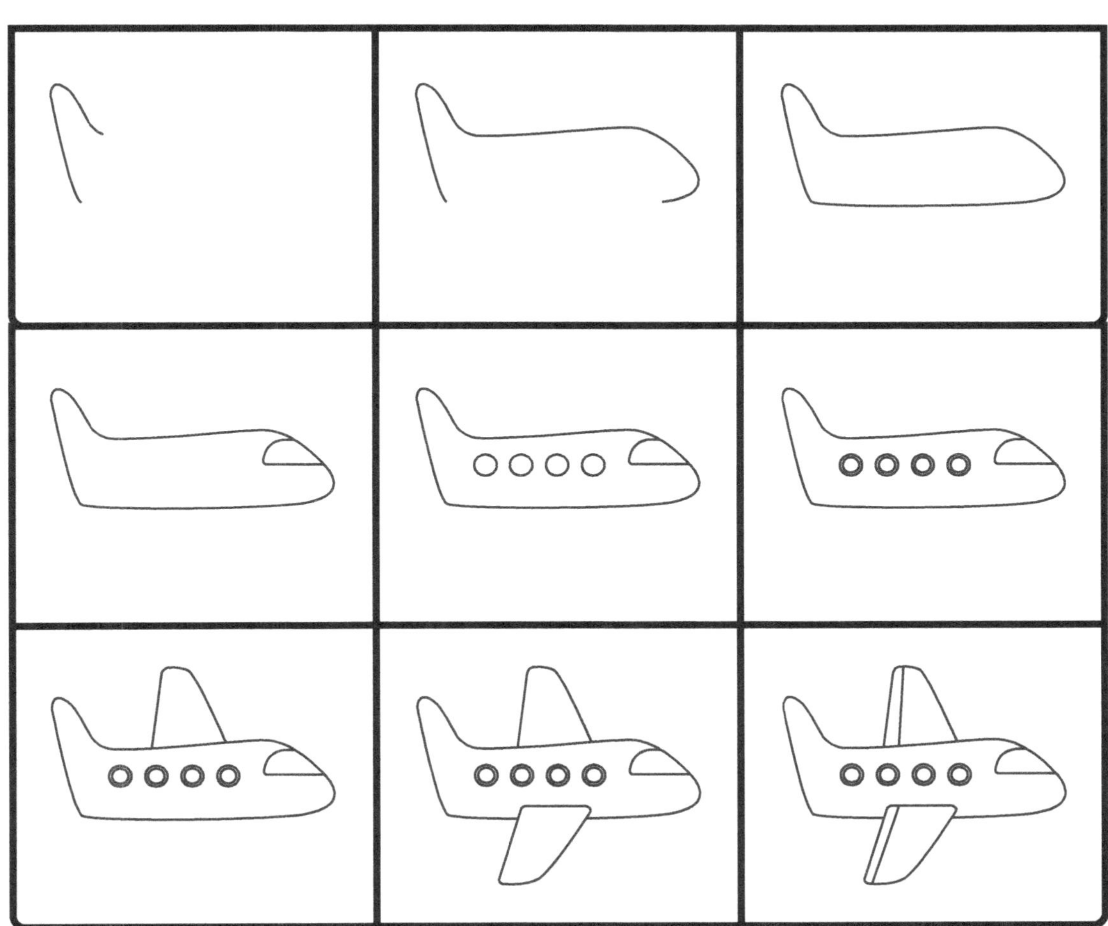

HELICOPTER

MAIN USE OF VEHICLE:

TO MOVE TROOPS, SUPPLIES, FOR RESCUE.

WHERE IT WAS FIRST MADE:

AMERICA 1939

FACT ABOUT VEHICLE:

PEOPLE HAVE USED HELICOPTERS TO BREAK OUT OF JAIL!

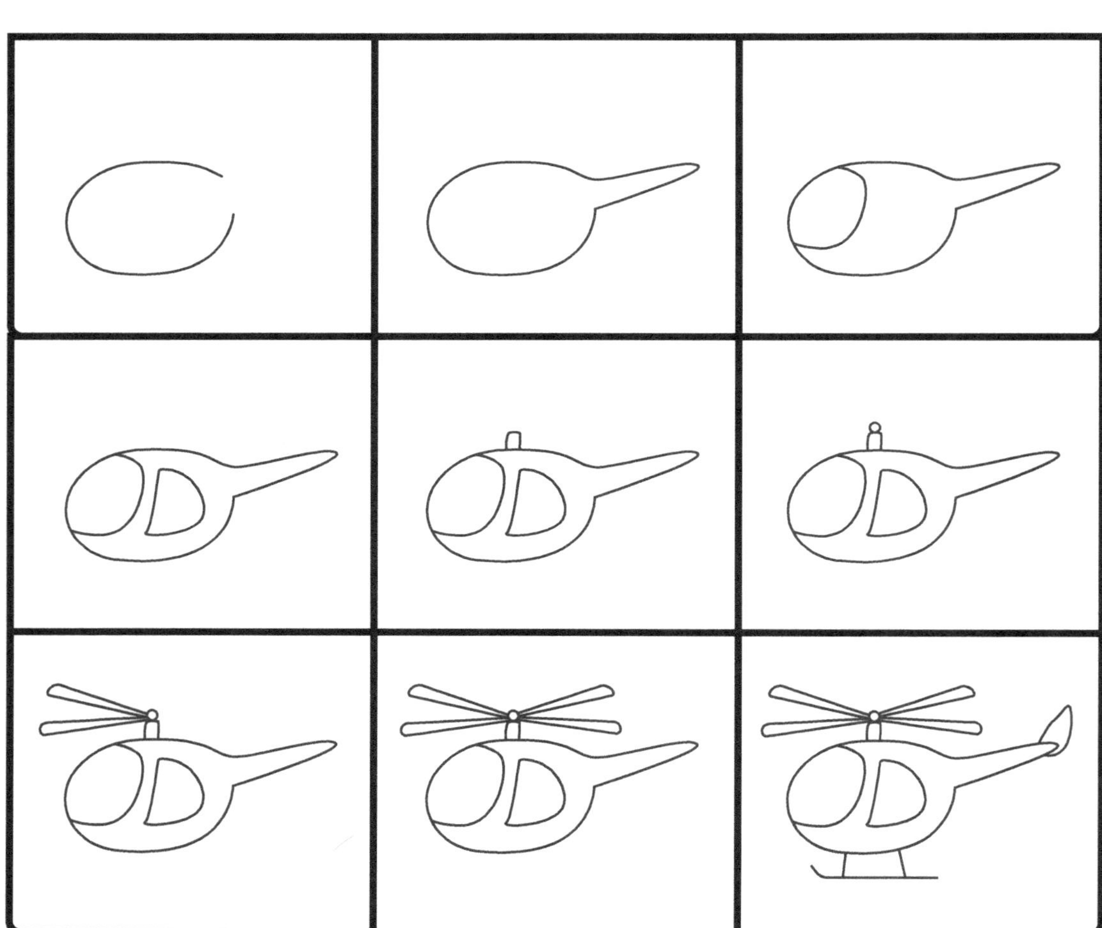

MAIN USE OF VEHICLE:
TO TRANSPORT PASSENGERS AND CARGO.

WHERE IT WAS FIRST MADE:
ENGLAND 1804

FACT ABOUT VEHICLE:
BULLET TRAINS CAN GO SUPER-FAST - UP TO 300 MPH!

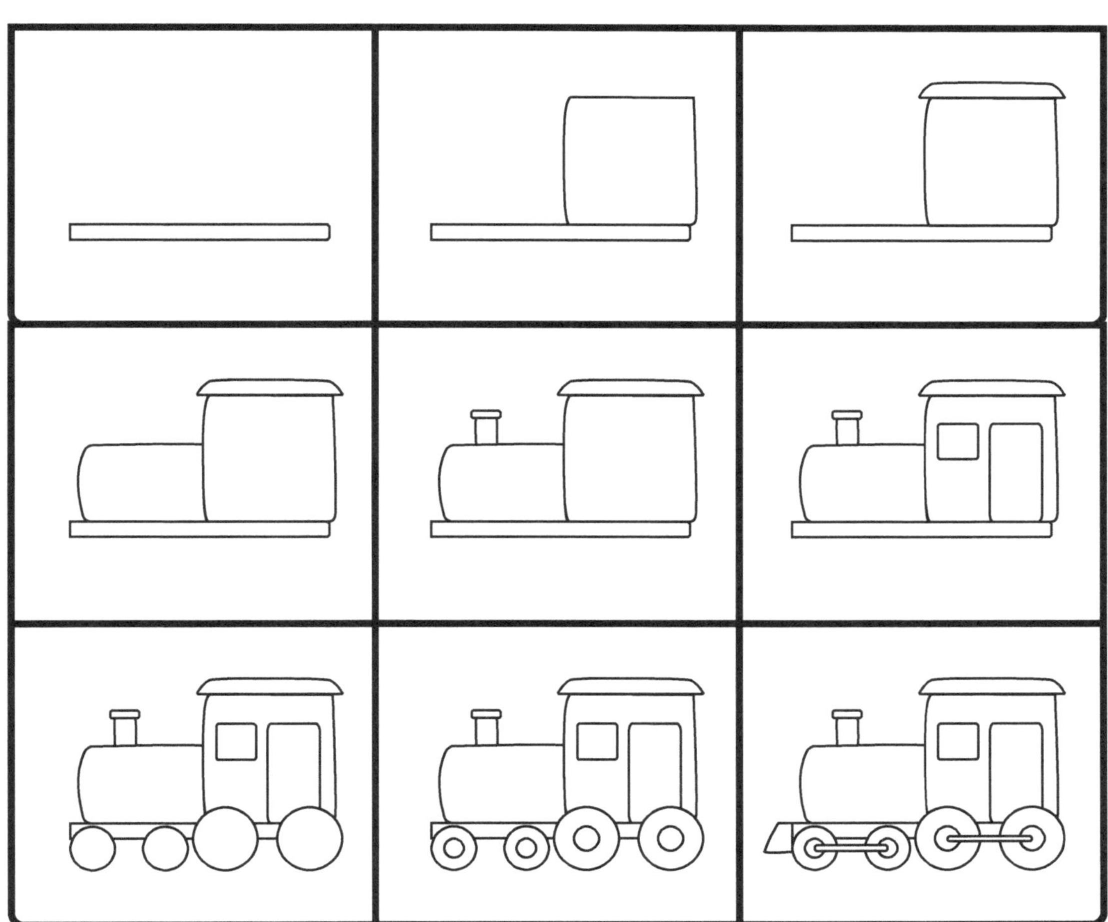

BUS

MAIN USE OF VEHICLE: TO TRANSPORT LARGE GROUPS OF PEOPLE.

WHERE IT WAS FIRST MADE: ENGLAND 1830.

FACT ABOUT VEHICLE: THE WORD 'BUS' IS ACTUALLY A SHORTENED VERSION OF 'OMNIBUS'.

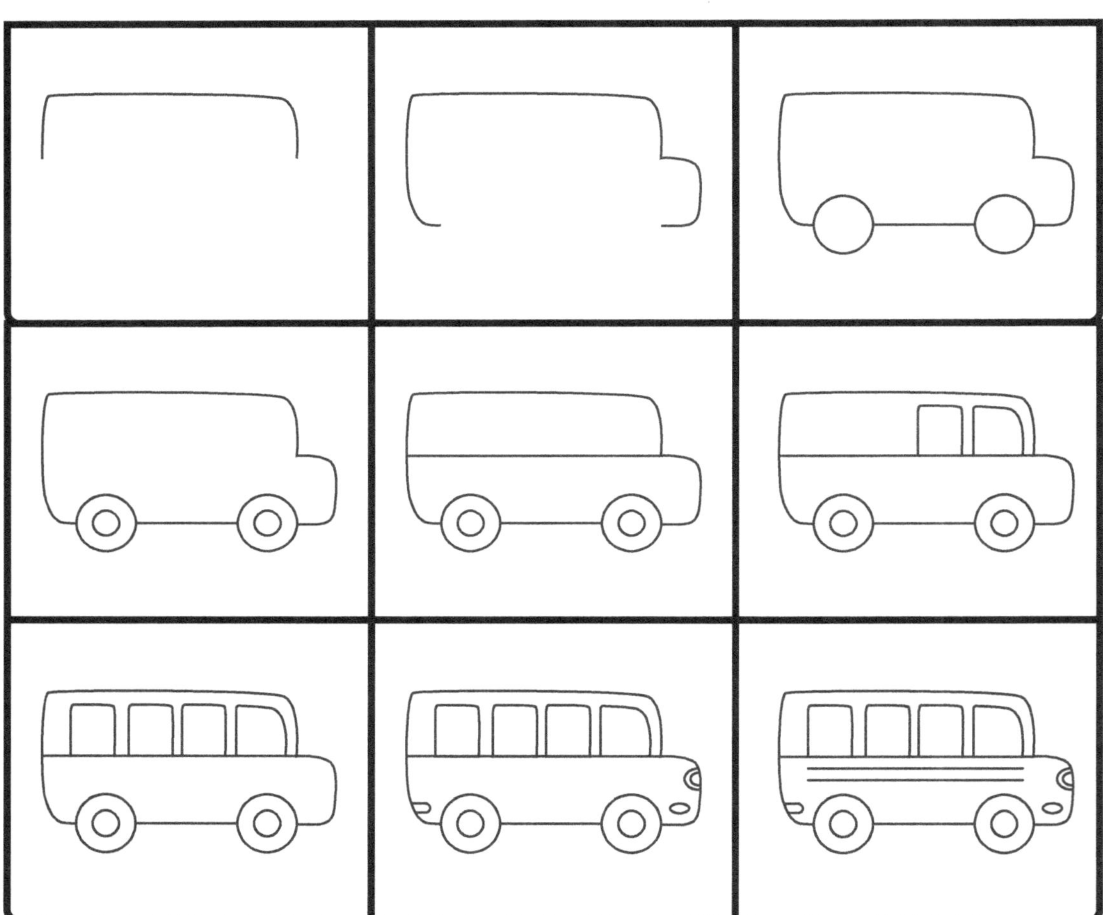

QUAD BIKE

MAIN USE OF VEHICLE:

FARM WORK AND RECREATION.

WHERE IT WAS FIRST MADE:

AMERICA 1980

FACT ABOUT VEHICLE:

PEOPLE CAN DO BACKFLIPS ON THEM!

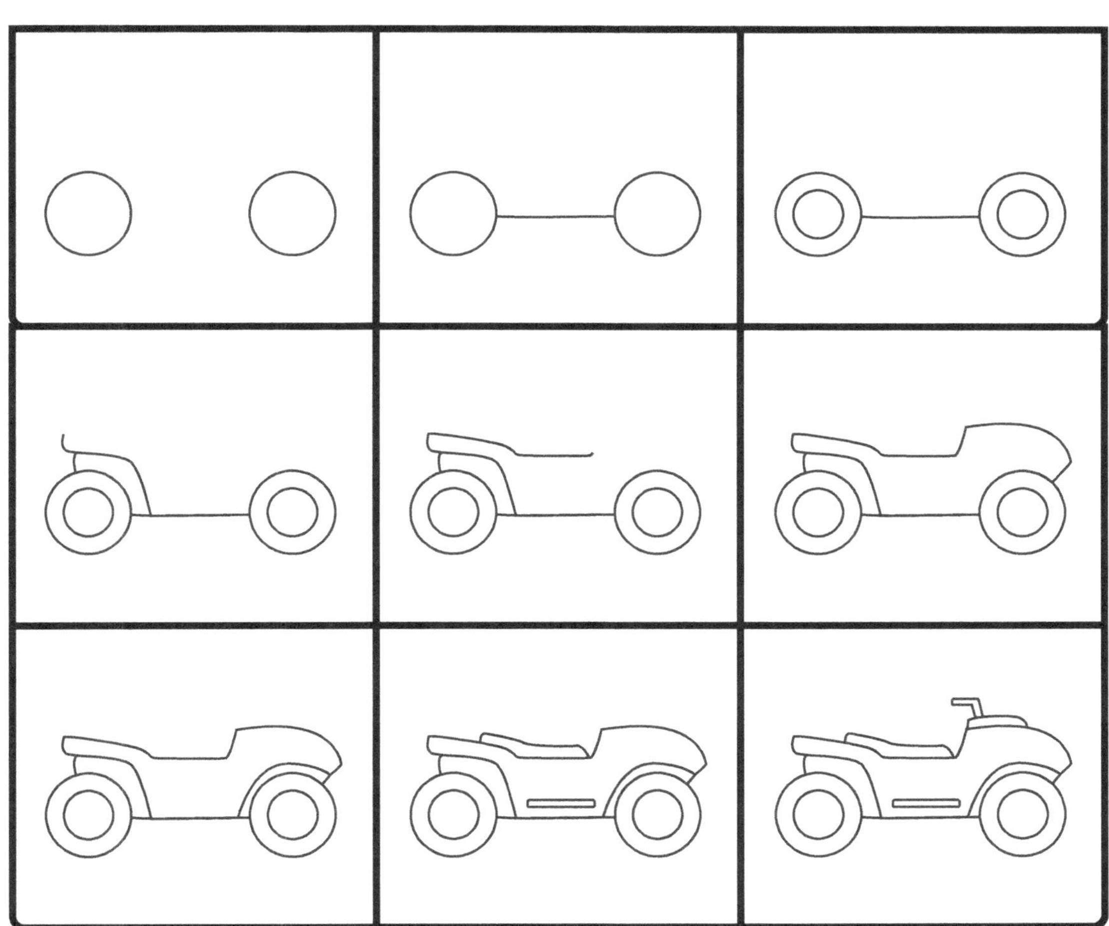

ROCKET SHIP

TO FLY INTO SPACE!

AMERICA 1926

ROCKET SHIPS ARE EXTREMELY HOT.

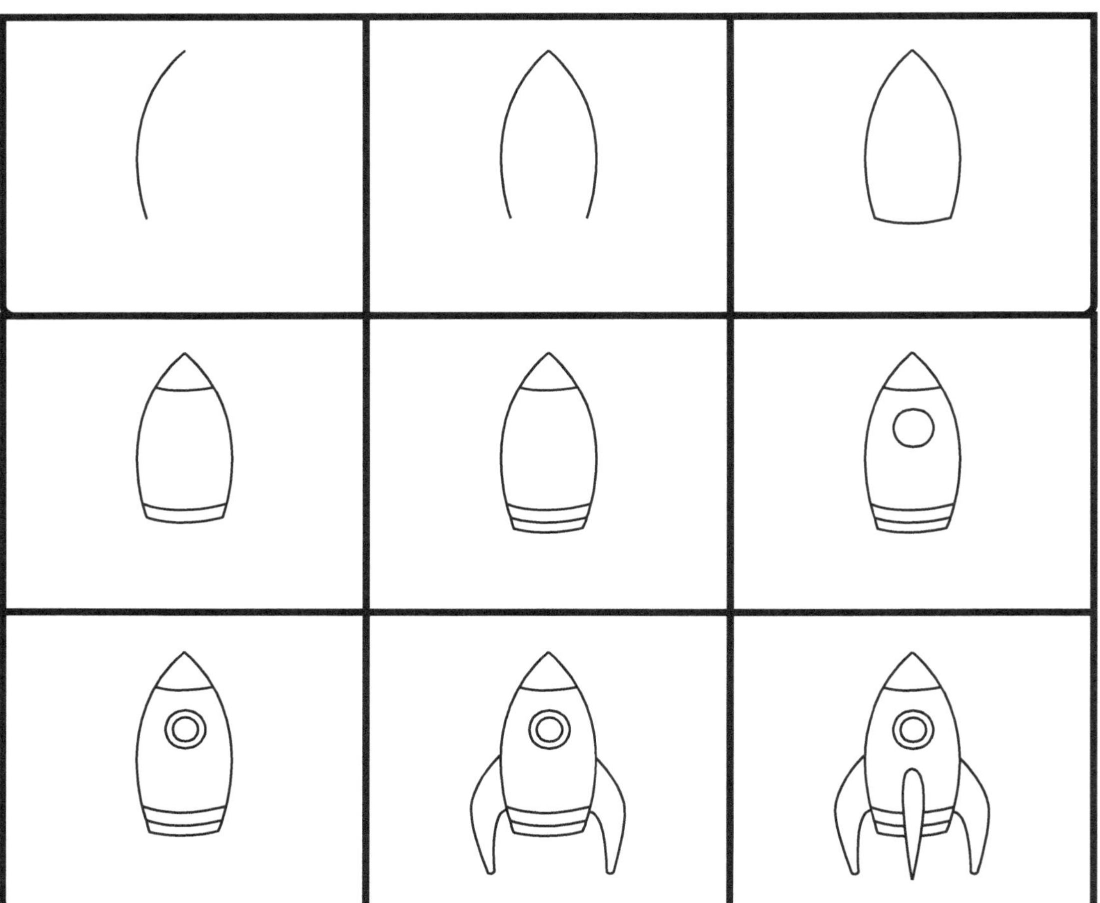

JET

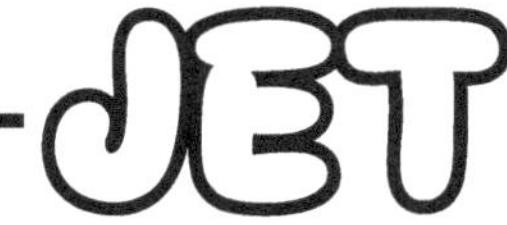

TO MOVE PEOPLE AROUND SUPER-FAST/FOR COMBAT.

GERMANY 1939

THEY ARE EXPENSIVE! AND COST BETWEEN $10-$40 MILLION.

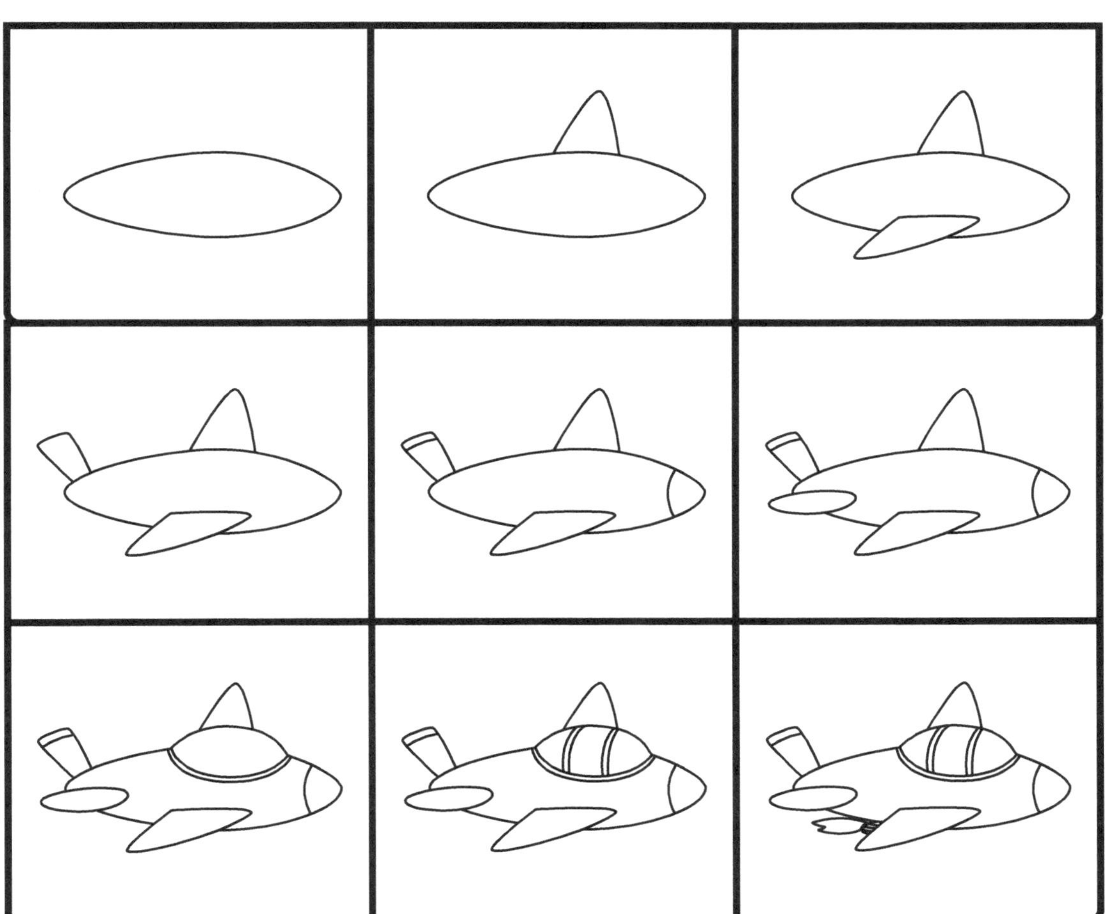

BICYCLE

MAIN USE OF VEHICLE:
TO GET ABOUT FASTER THAN WALKING, AND TO TRANSPORT SMALL GOODS.

WHERE IT WAS FIRST MADE:
GERMANY 1817

FACT ABOUT VEHICLE:
THE LONGEST TANDEM BICYCLE CAN FIT 35 PEOPLE!

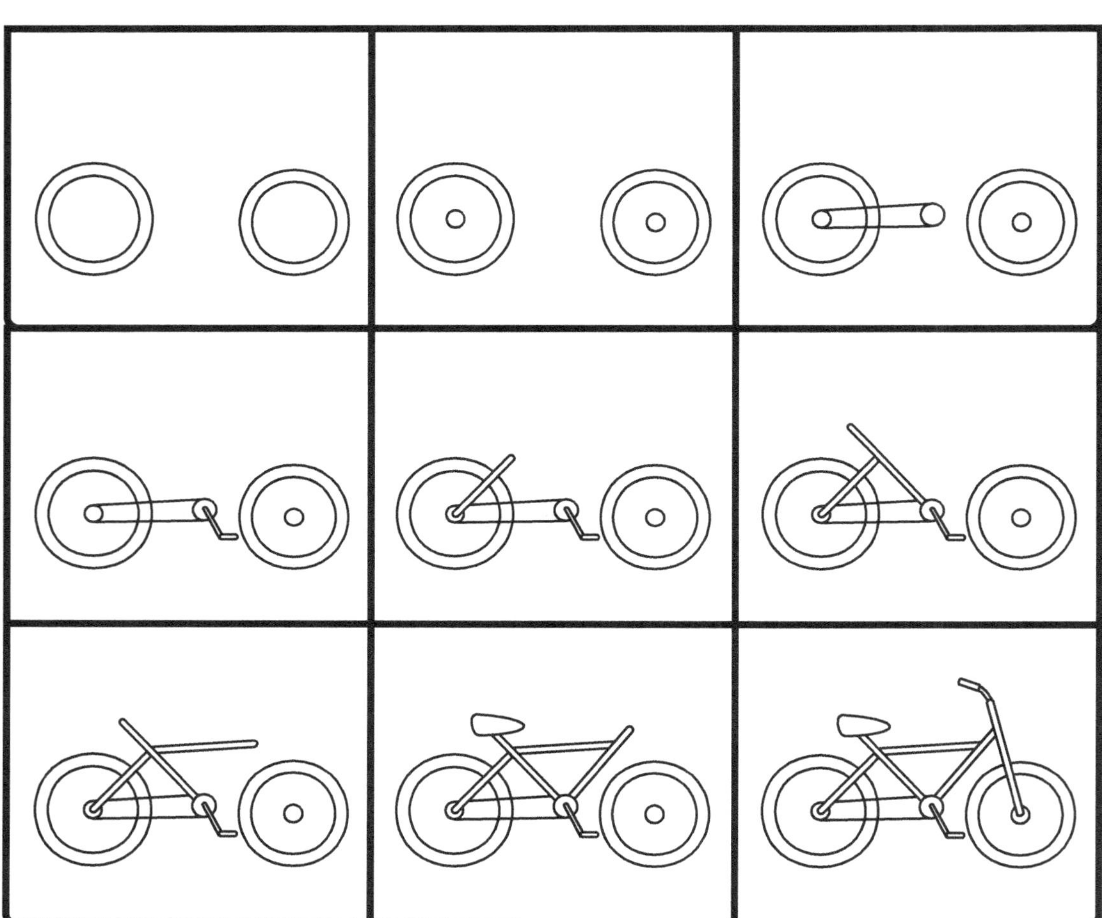

CRANE

TO LIFT AND MOVE HEAVY LOADS.

IRAQ 3000 BC

CRANES ARE NAMED AFTER THE 'CRANE' BIRD!

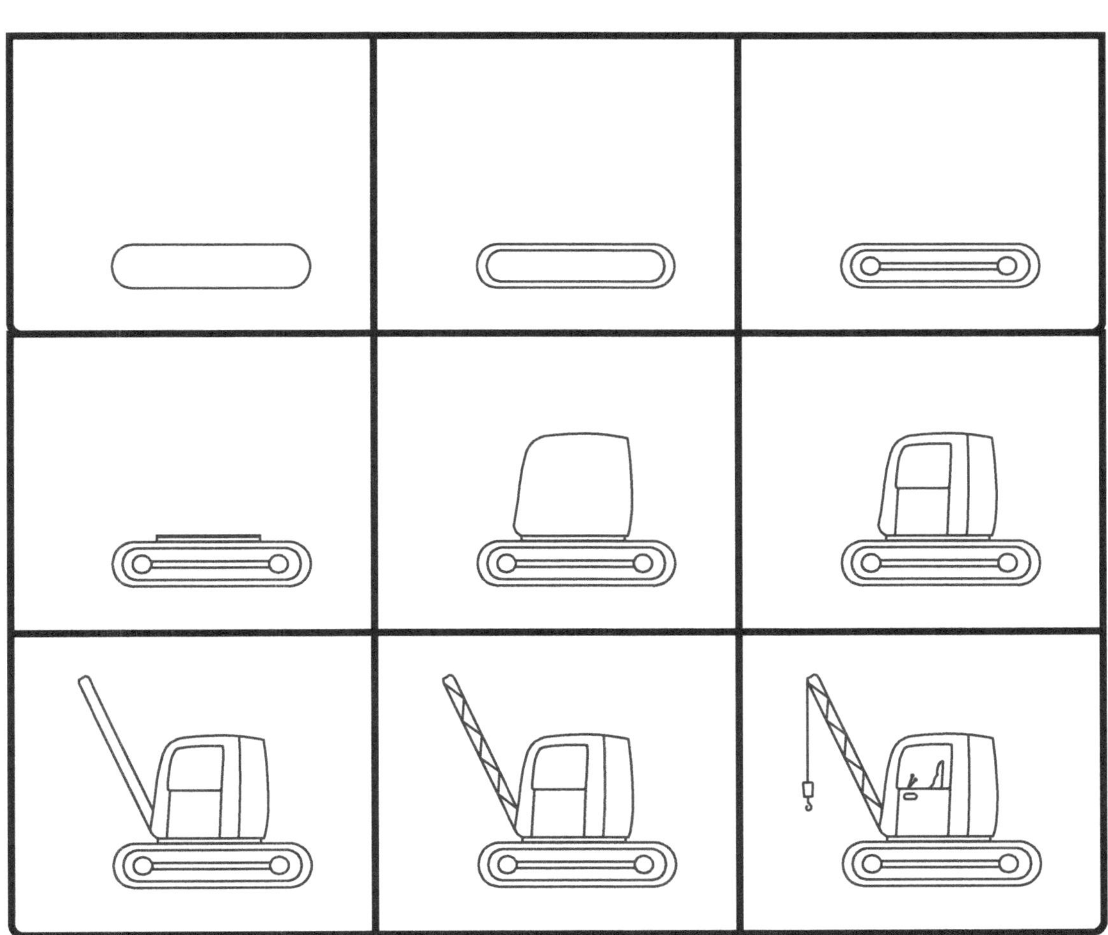

SPORTS CAR

MAIN USE OF VEHICLE:
RECREATION.

WHERE IT WAS FIRST MADE:
ENGLAND 1914

FACT ABOUT VEHICLE:
THE FASTEST SPORTSCAR (THE BUGATTI VEYRON SUPERSPORT) CAN GO 268 MPH.

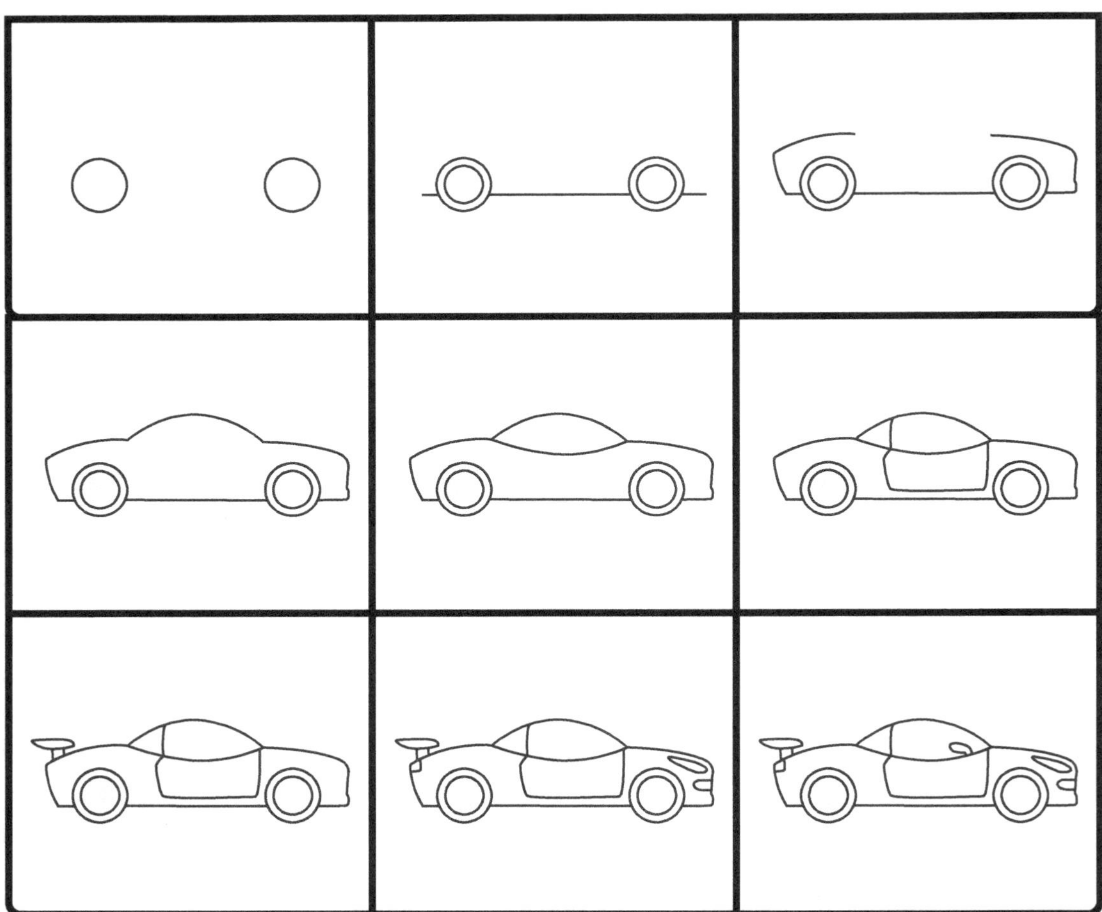

UFO

MAIN USE OF VEHICLE:	WHERE IT WAS FIRST MADE:	FACT ABOUT VEHICLE:
TO FLY IN SPACE.	UNKNOWN.	5% - 20% OF UFOS ARE UNEXPLAINED.

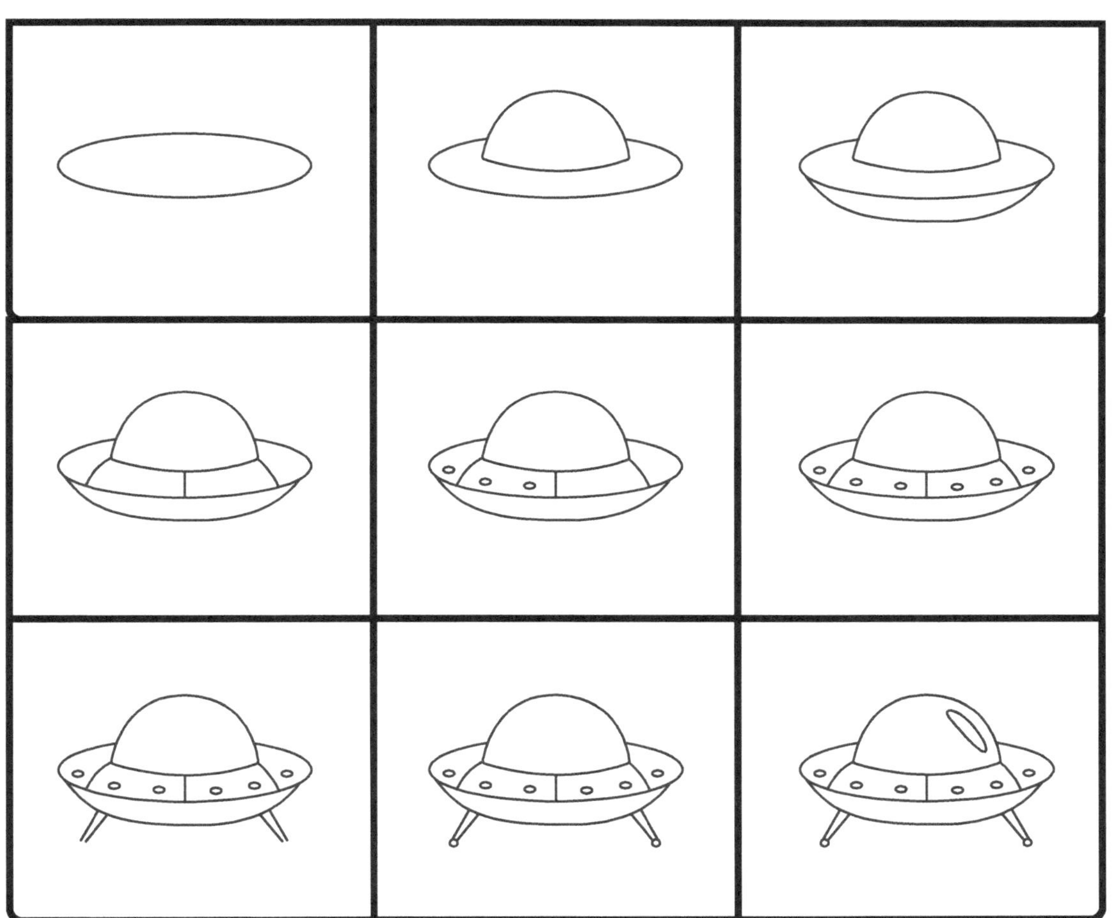

HOT AIR BALLOON

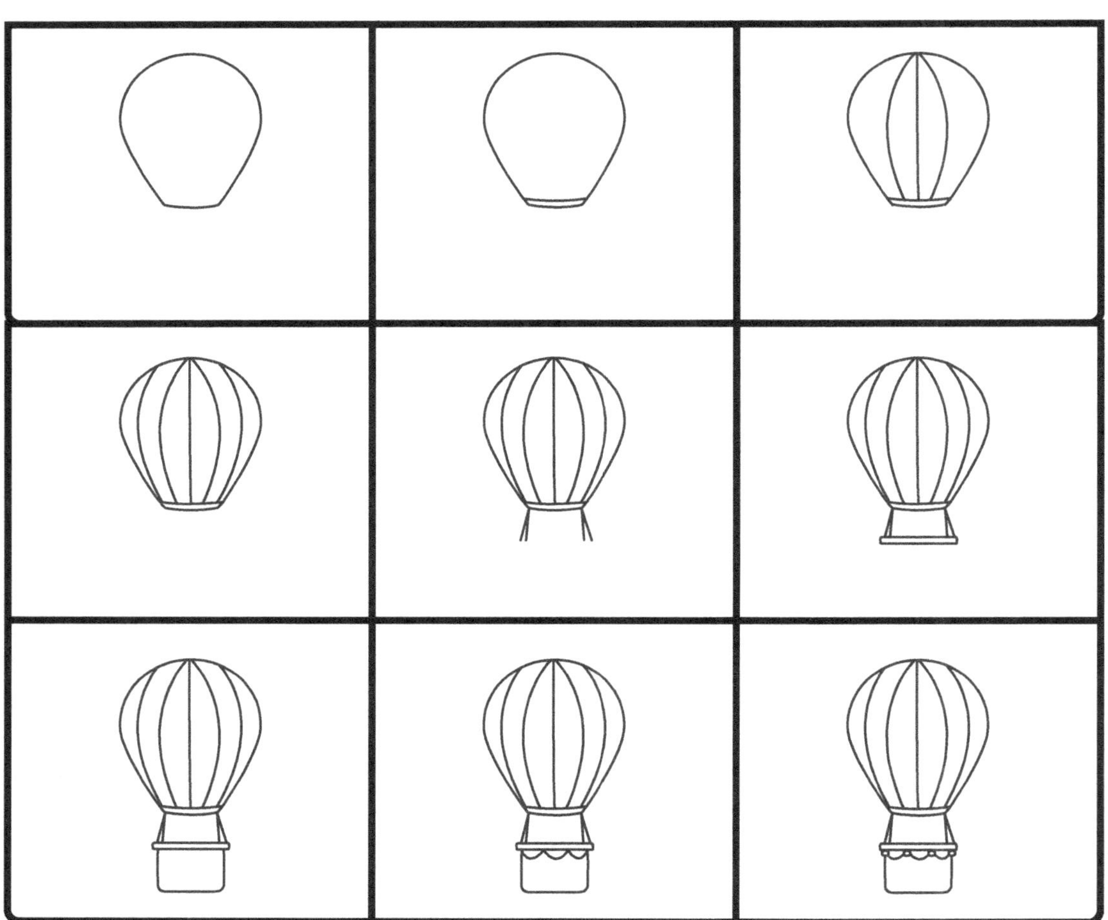

ATV

MAIN USE OF VEHICLE:
TO GET ABOUT IN DIFFERENT/ DIFFICULT TERRAINS.

WHERE IT WAS FIRST MADE:
CANADA 1967.

FACT ABOUT VEHICLE:
SOME OF THE FIRST ATVS HAD SIX WHEELS.

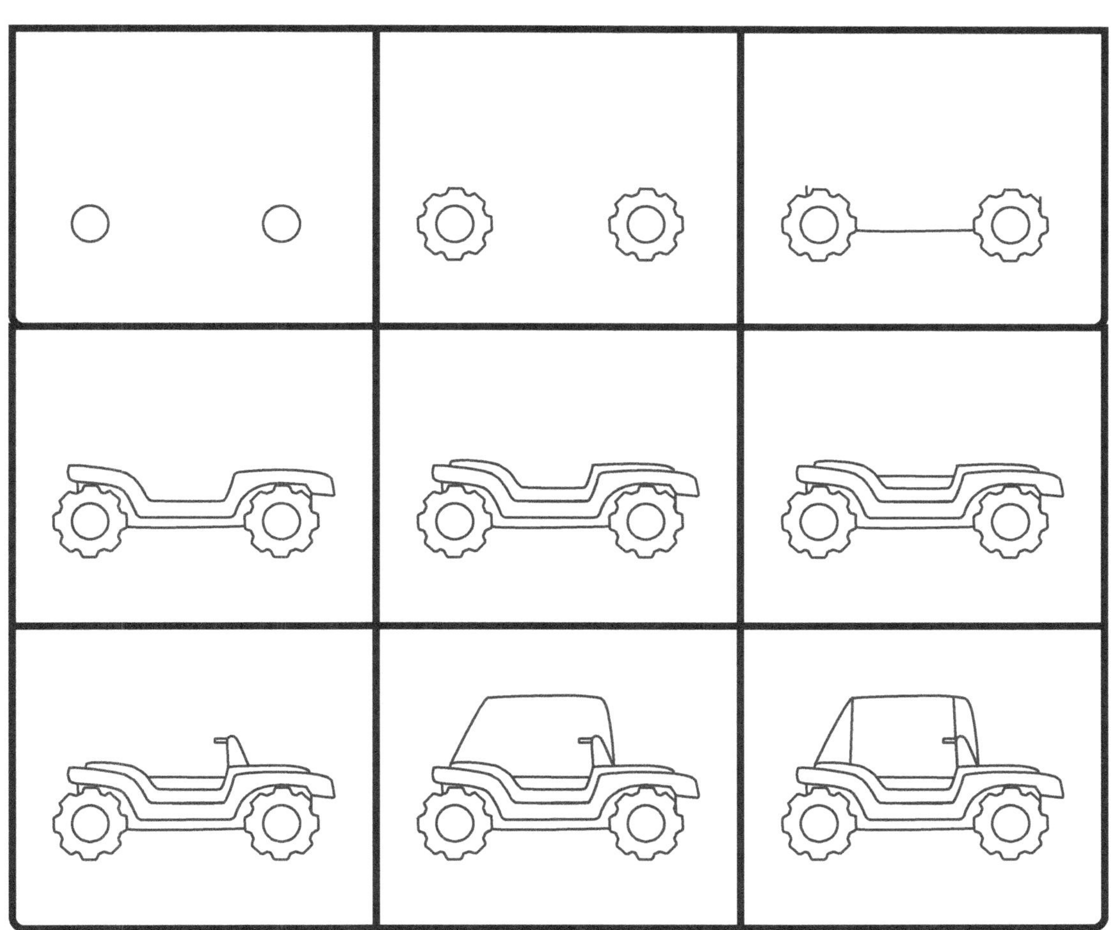

JETSKI

MAIN USE OF VEHICLE:
RECREATIONS - TO GET ABOUT FAST ON THE WATER.

WHERE IT WAS FIRST MADE:
AMERICAN 1972.

FACT ABOUT VEHICLE:
YOU CAN DO TRICKS ON A JETSKI.

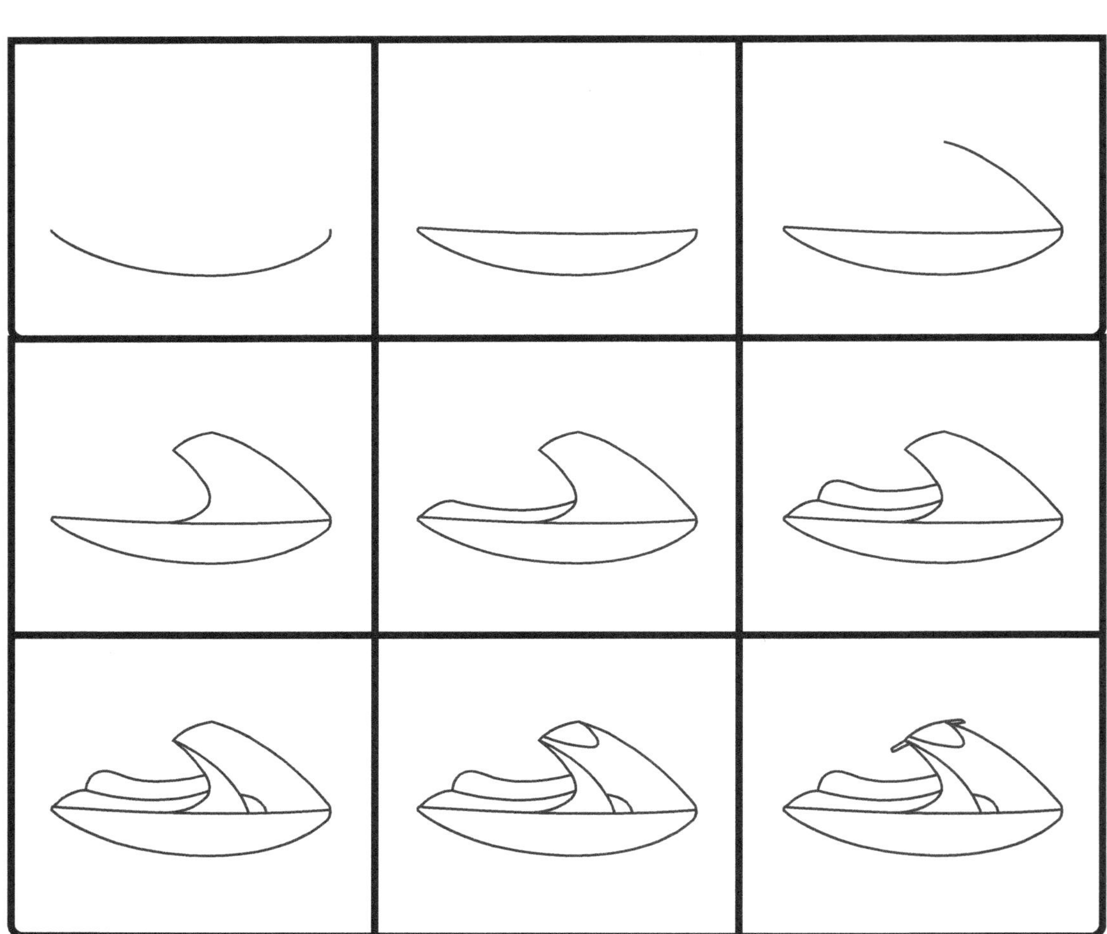

PARACHUTE

MAIN USE OF VEHICLE:

TO ALLOW PEOPLE TO FALL FROM THE AIR GENTLY AND SAFELY.

WHERE IT WAS FIRST MADE:

FRANCE 1783

FACT ABOUT VEHICLE:

TO SAFELY STOP AND LAND THE SPACE SHUTTE, NASA USED A PARACHUTE.

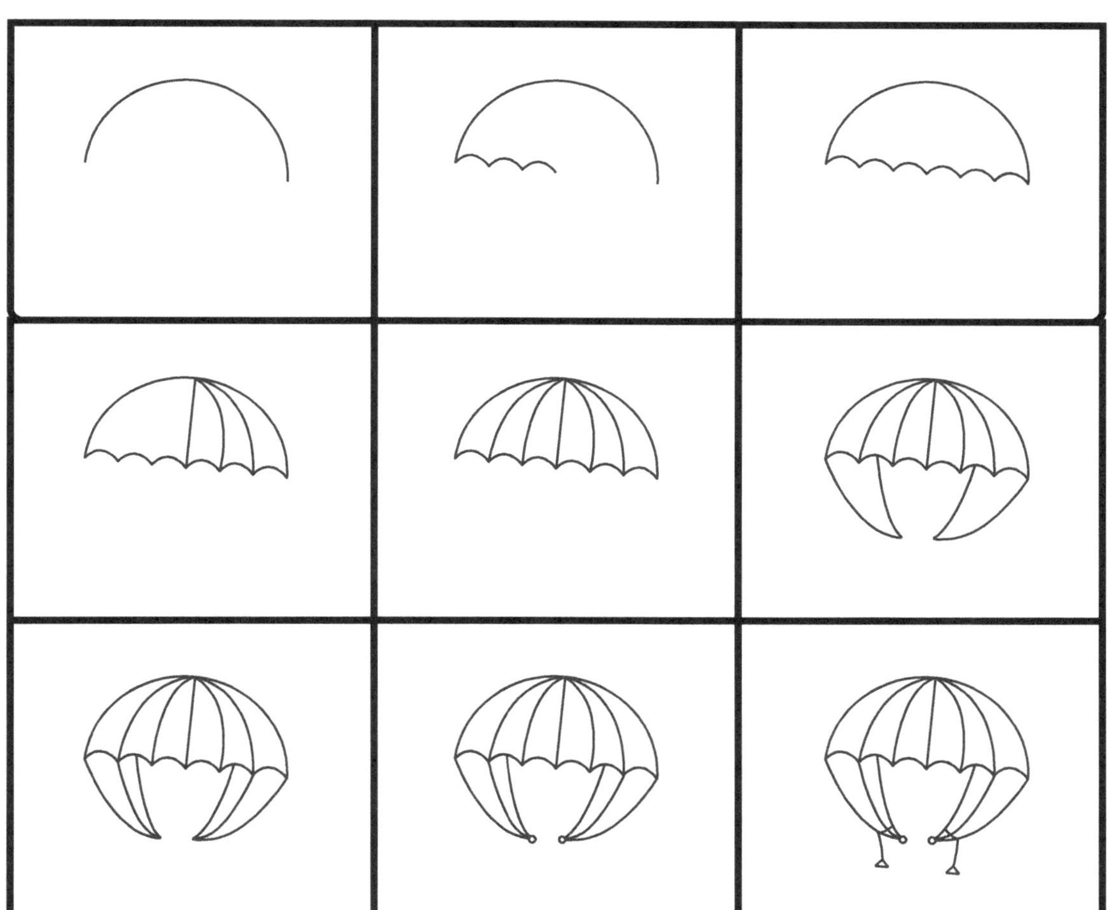

SUBMARINE

MAIN USE OF VEHICLE:
TO BE HIDDEN IN WAR AND FOR MARINE SCIENCE.

WHERE IT WAS FIRST MADE:
ENGLAND 17TH CENTURY.

FACT ABOUT VEHICLE:
SUBMARINES FLUSH THEIR TOILETS WITH SEAWATER.

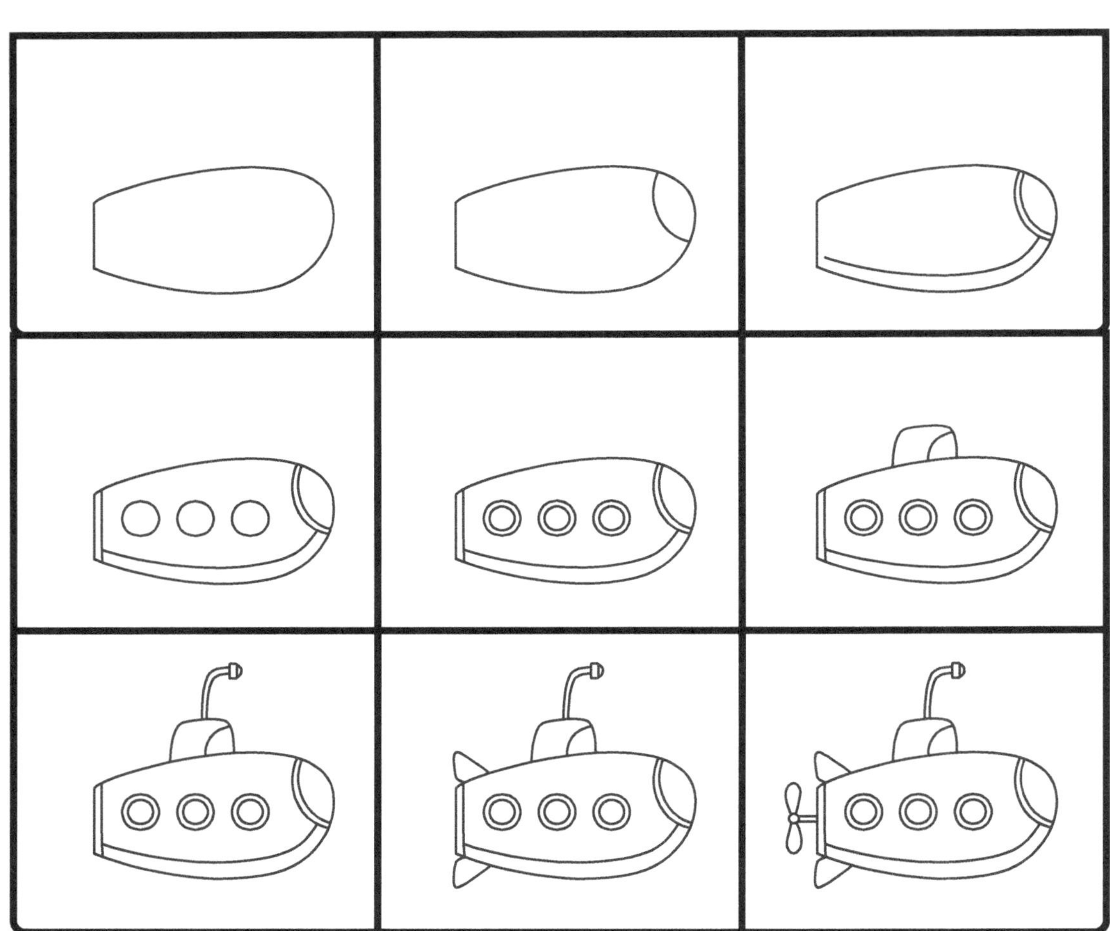

SURFBOARD

TO RIDE AN OCEAN WAVE.

AMERICA 1926

EVEN DOGS CAN ENTER SURFING COMPETITIONS!

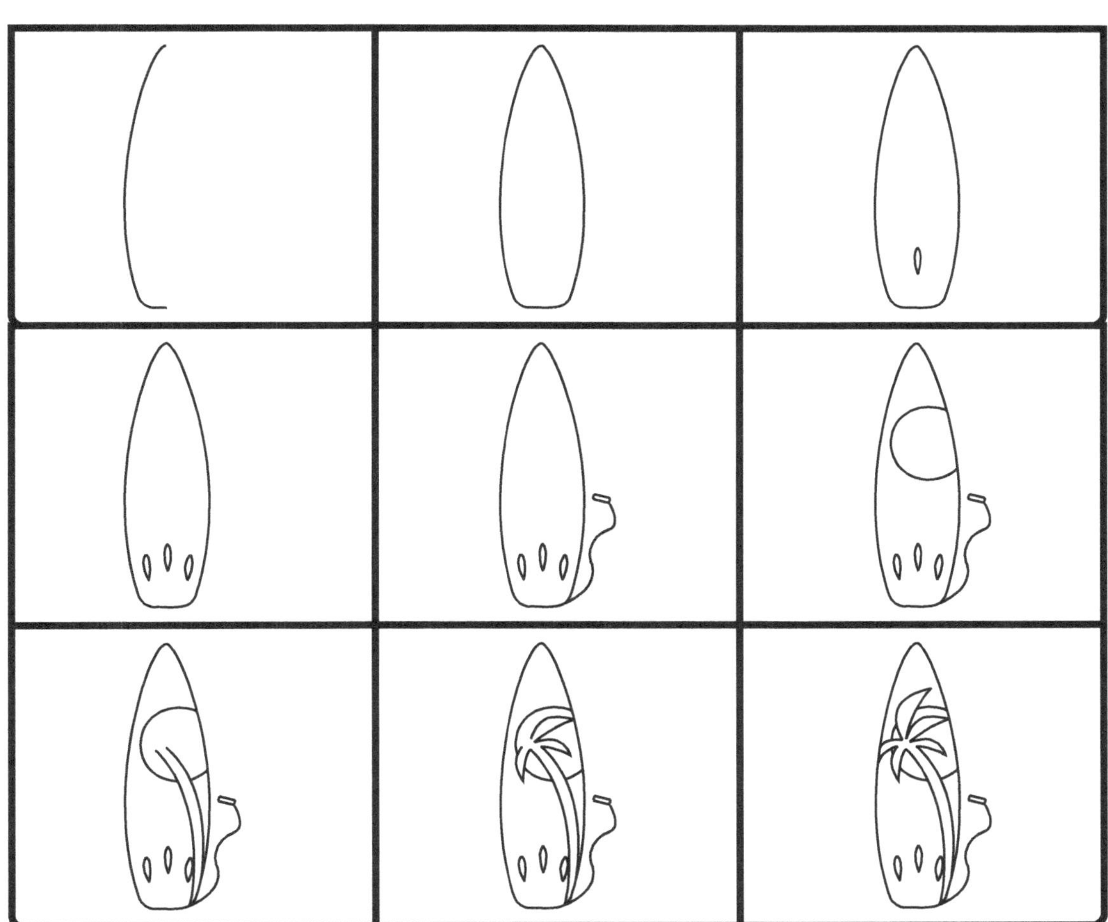

MONSTER TRUCK

ENTERTAINMENT.

AMERICA 1982

MONSTER TRUCKS CAN JUMP OVER UP TO 14 CARS!

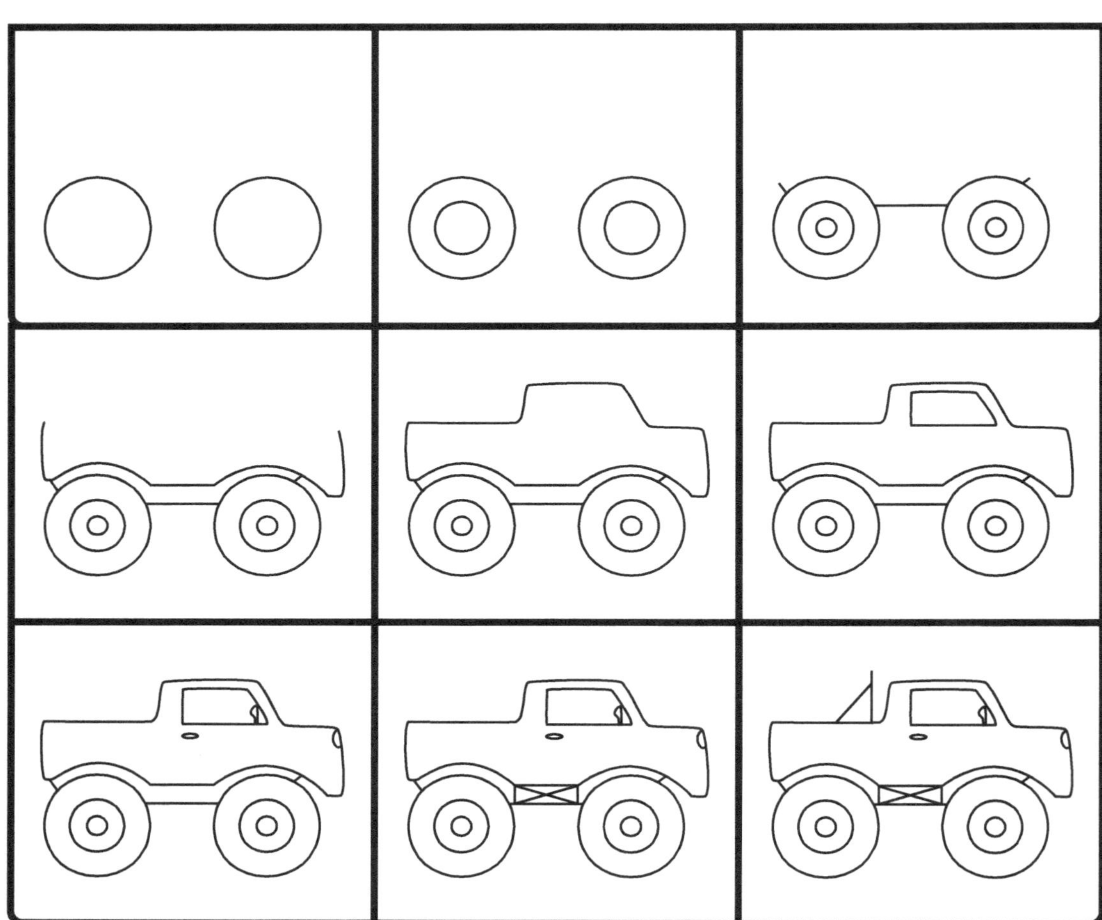

SHIP

MAIN USE OF VEHICLE:
TO CARRY CARGO AND PEOPLE LONG DISTANCES.

WHERE IT WAS FIRST MADE:
ANCIENT EGYPT.

FACT ABOUT VEHICLE:
THE LARGEST SHIPS CAN CARRY UP TO 20,000 CONTAINERS.

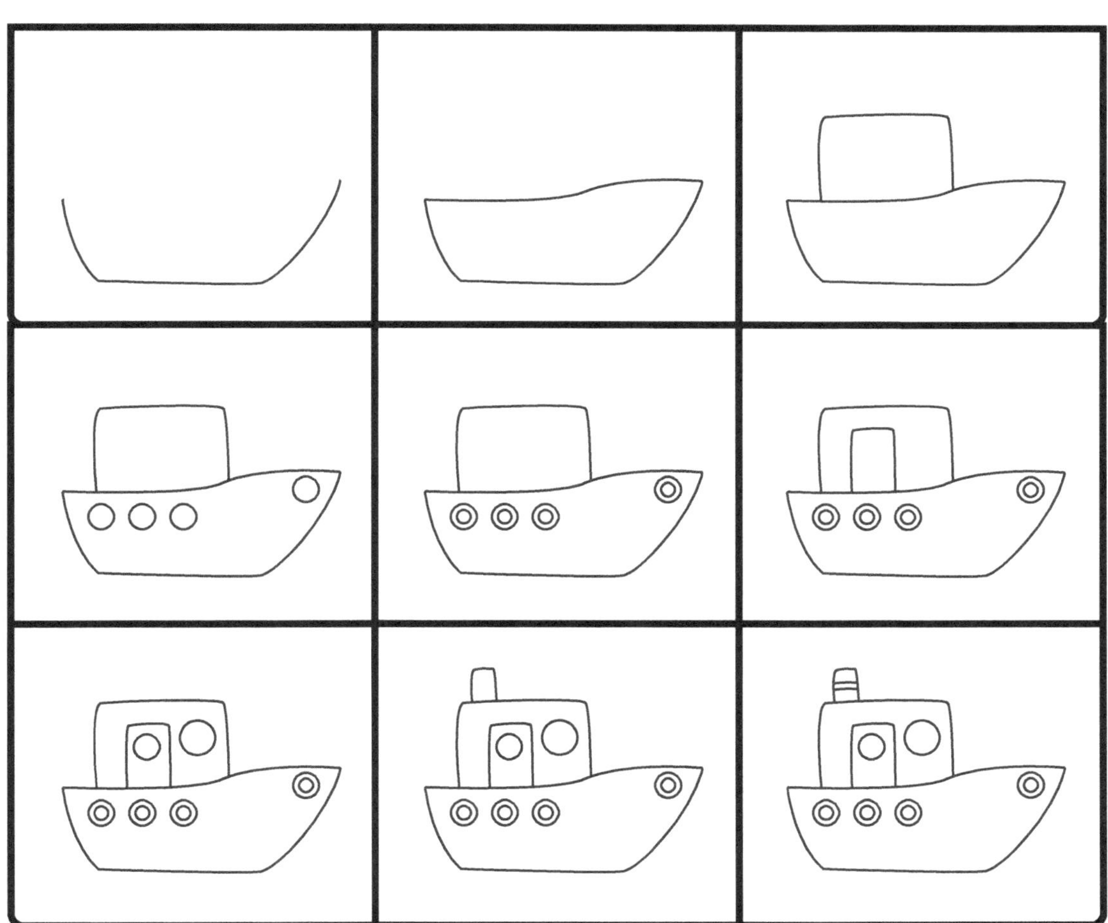

SAILBOAT

TO SAIL ACROSS THE WATER.

ANCIENT EGYPT.

SAILING HAS BEEN A PART OF THE OLYMPICS SINCE 1896.

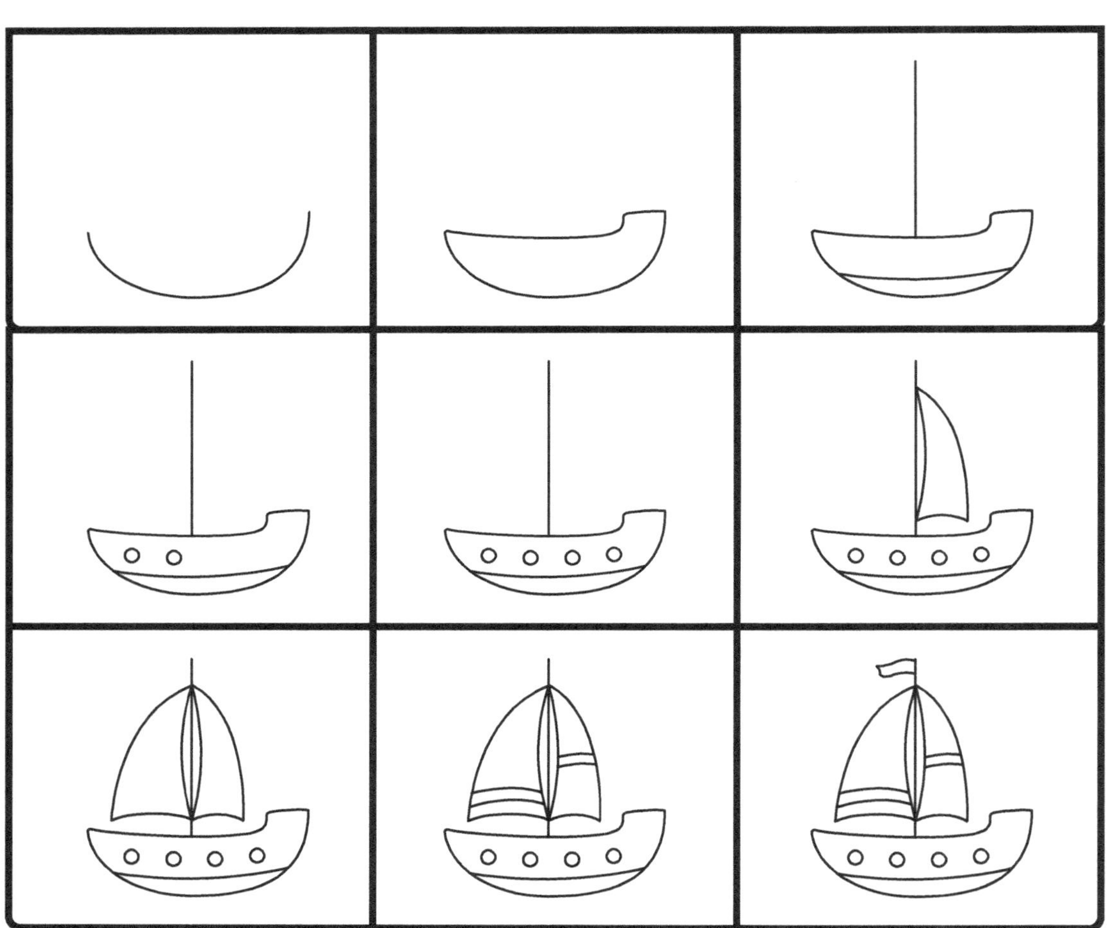

TRACTOR

MAIN USE OF VEHICLE:

FOR FARMING -
PLOUGHING AND
PLANTING FIELDS.

WHERE IT WAS
FIRST MADE:

AMERICA 1892.

FACT ABOUT VEHICLE:

TRACTORS CAN
ACTUALLY GO
QUITE FAST!

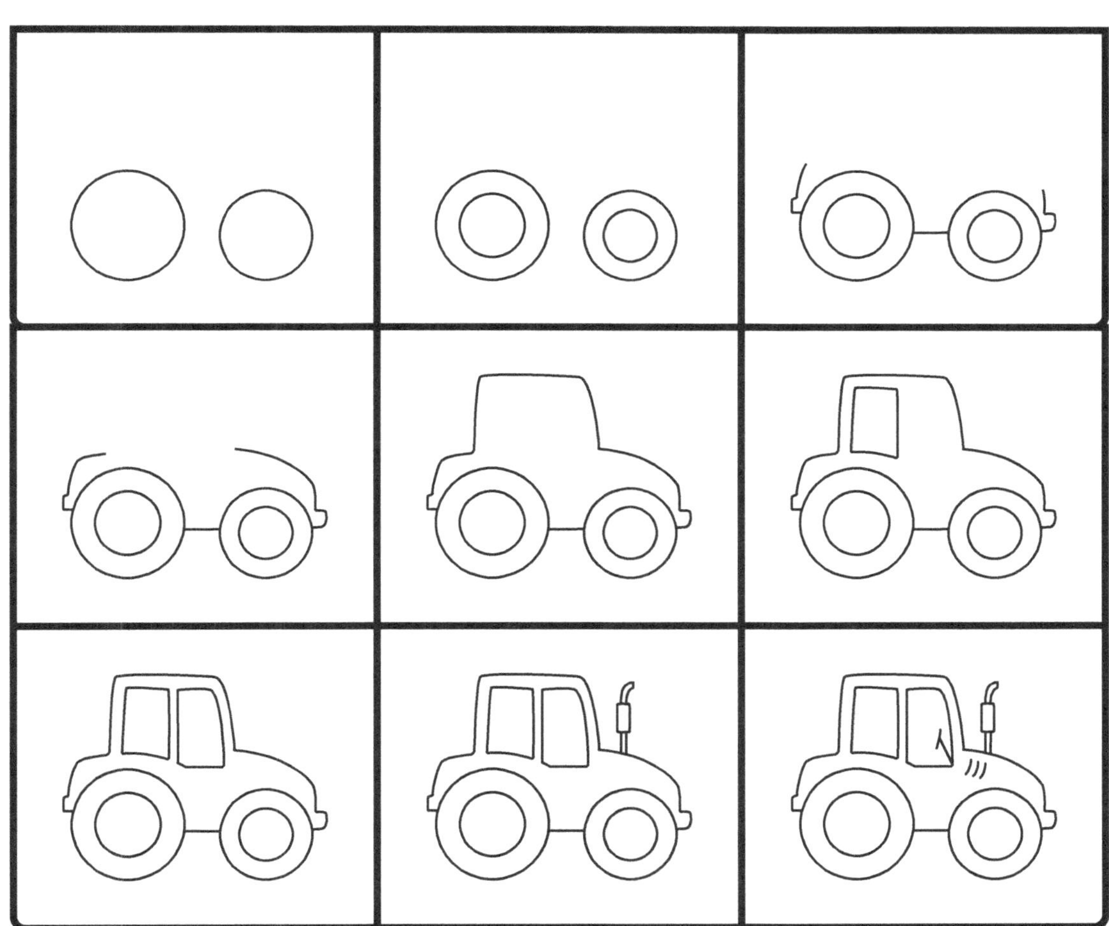

SKATEBOARD

FUN AND SPORT.

AMERICA 1959.

BEFORE SKATE RINKS AND RAMPS WERE INTRODUCED PEOPLE PRACTICED IN EMPTY SWIMMING POOLS AND DRAINAGE DITCHES.

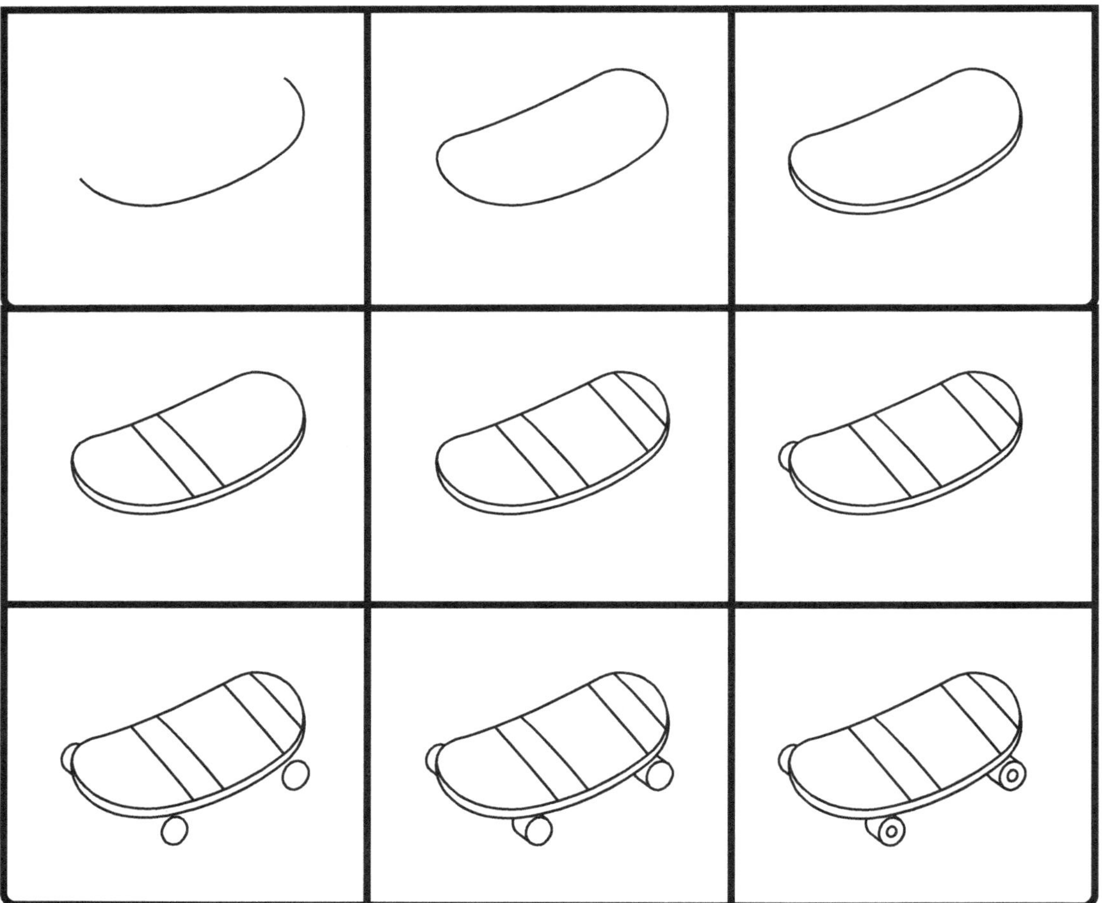

SCOOTER

FUN! AND TO GET ABOUT QUICKLY AND EASILY.

BY KIDS DURING THE GREAT DEPRESSION!

KIDS BORED OF THEIR ROLLER-SKATES ATTACHED A PLANT OF WOOD AND INVENTED THE ORIGINAL SCOOTER.

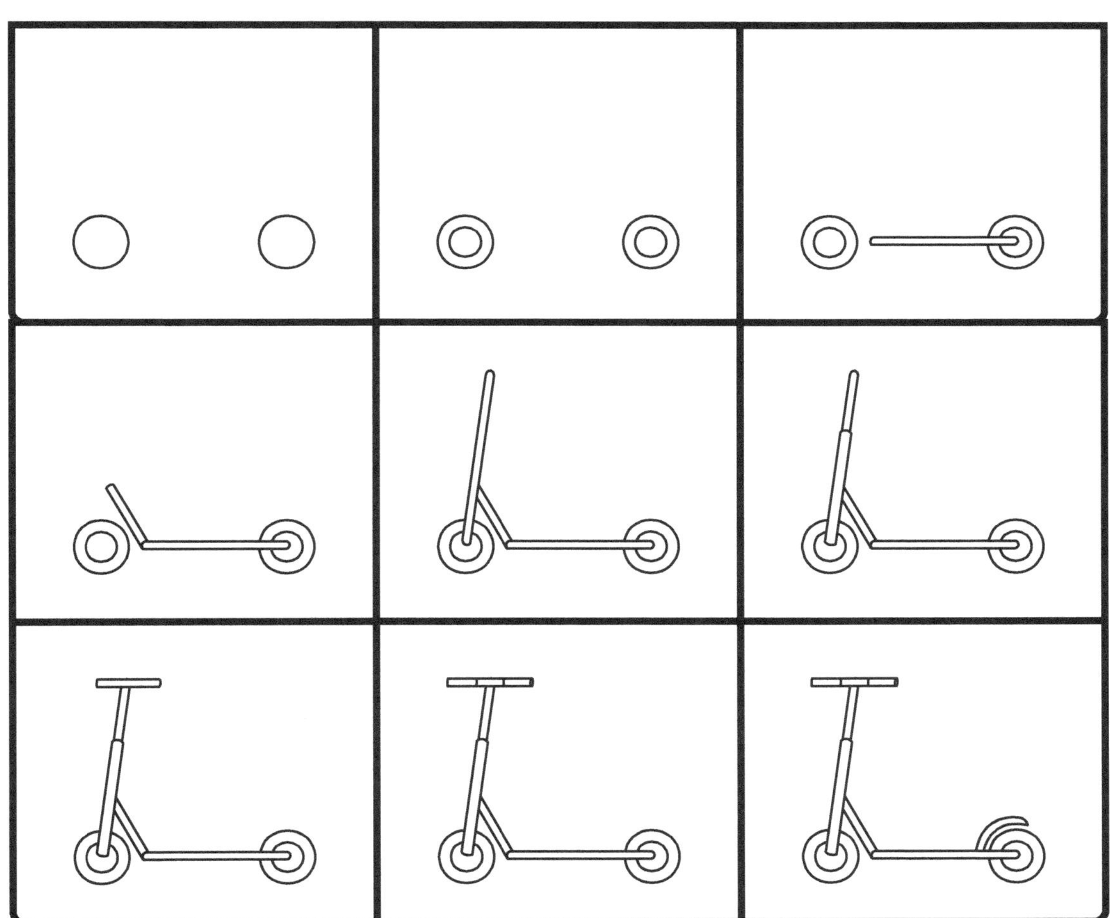

BULLDOZER

MAIN USE OF VEHICLE: DIGGING AND SPREADING SOIL.

WHERE IT WAS FIRST MADE: AMERICA 1923.

FACT ABOUT VEHICLE: THE FIRST BULLDOZERS WERE MADE FROM ADAPTED TRACTORS USED ON FARMS.

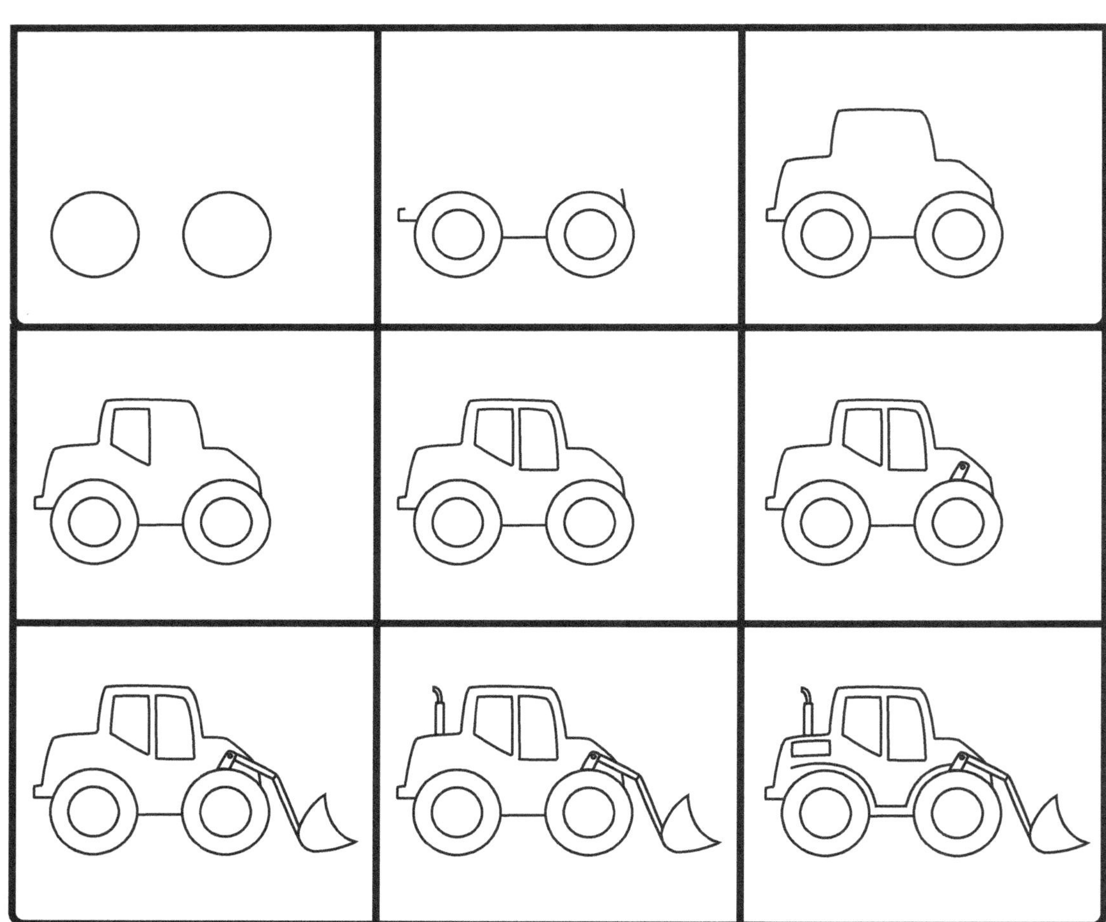

FIRETRUCK

MAIN USE OF VEHICLE:

TO TRANSPORT FIREFIGHTERS TO PUT OUT FIRES.

WHERE IT WAS FIRST MADE:

AMERICA 1743.

FACT ABOUT VEHICLE:

FIRE TRUCKS CAN CARRY AROUND 1000 TO 3700 LITRES OF WATER!

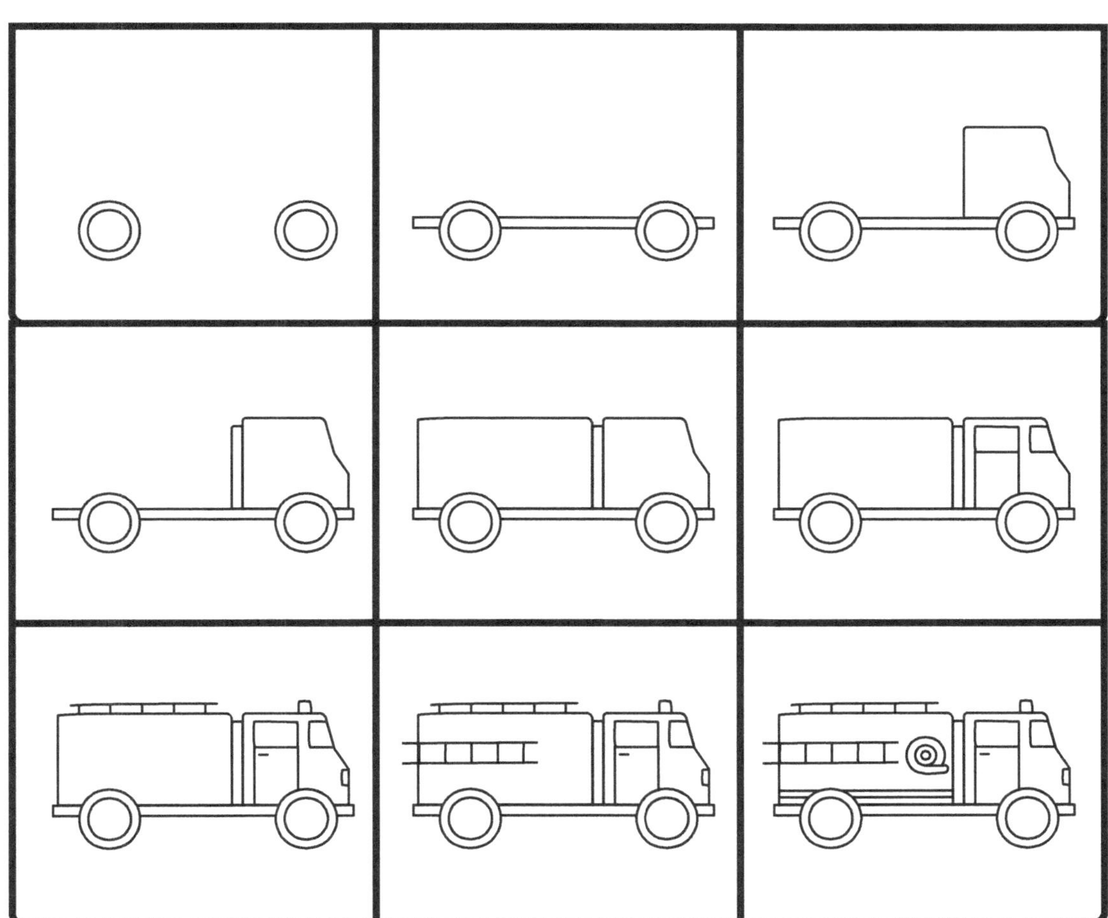

ROAD ROLLER

ROADWORK JOBS - FLATTENING SURFACES TO MAKE ROADS.

FRANCE 1863

THE FIRST ROAD ROLLERS WERE PULLED BY HORSES.

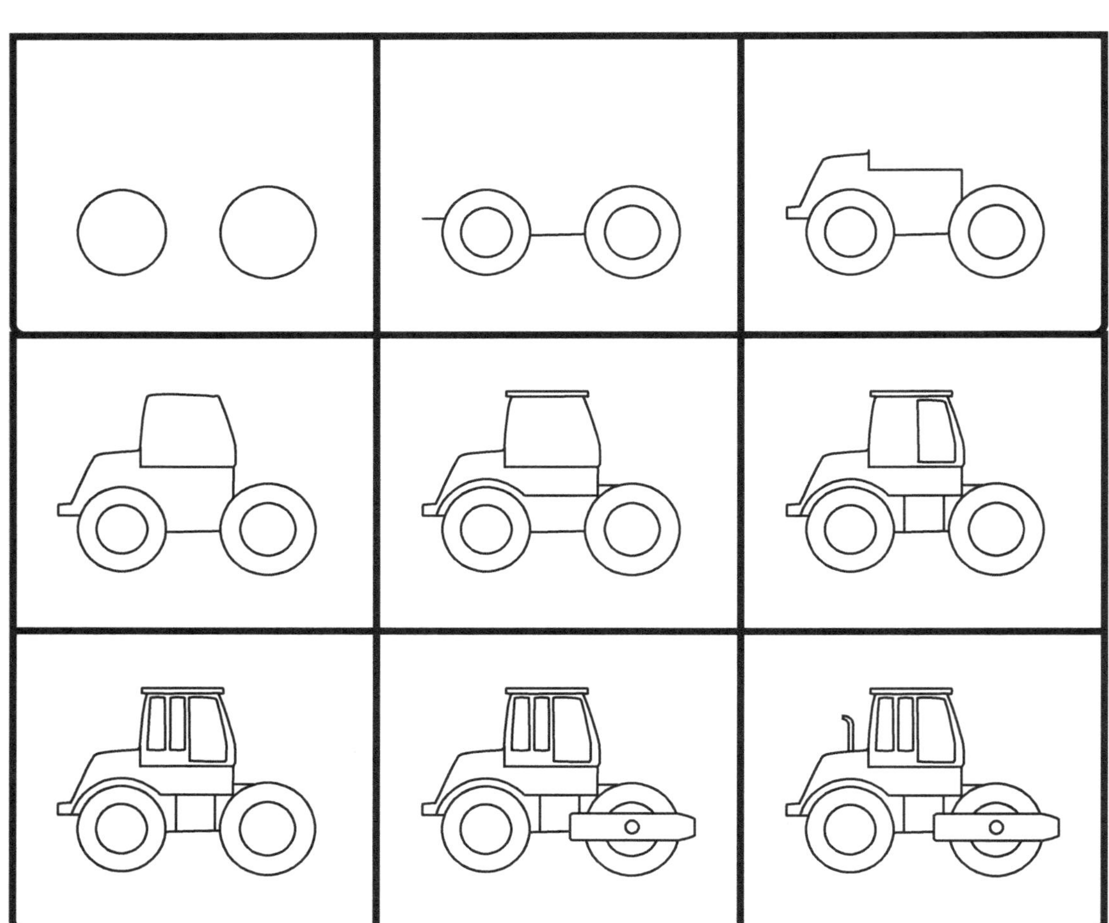

DUMP TRUCK

TO PICK UP RUBBISH AND TRANSPORT IT TO A TIP.

CANADA 1920.

DUMP TRUCKS WERE FIRST USED ON FARMS.

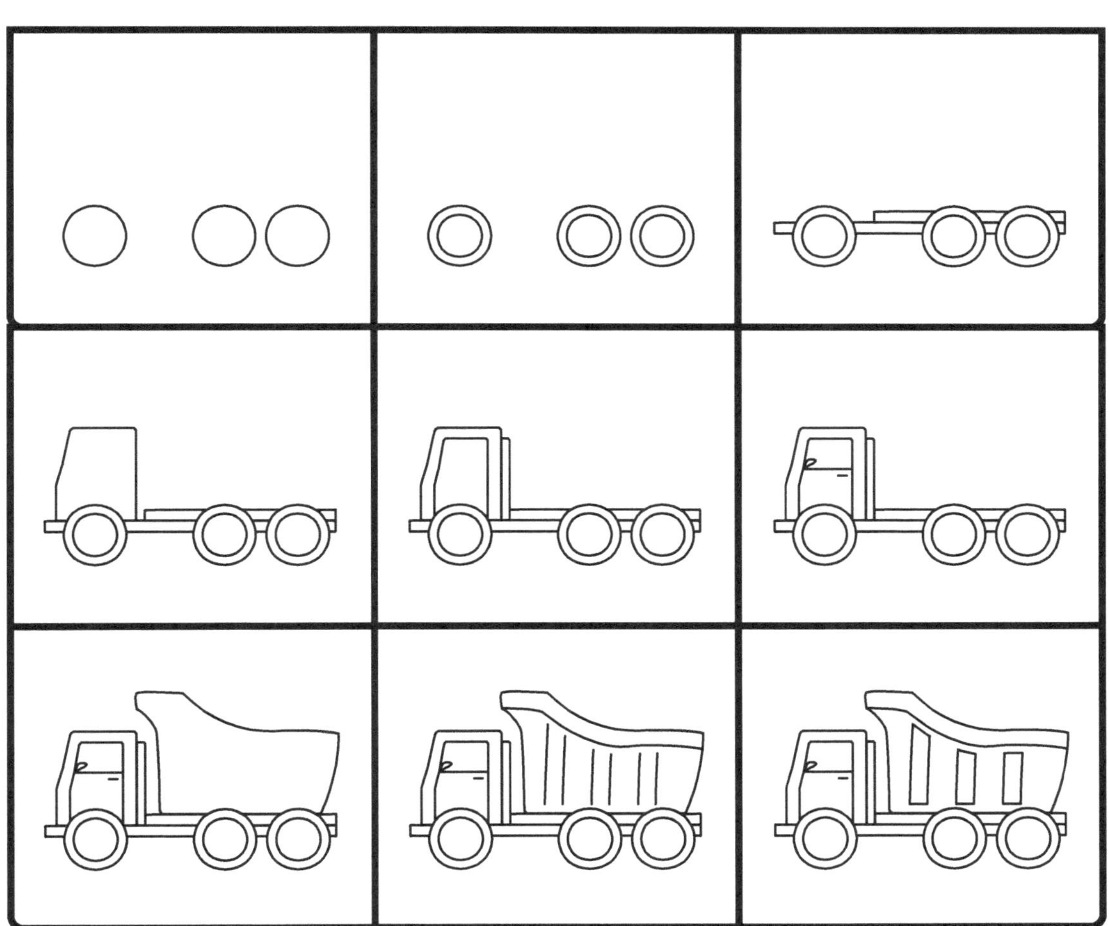

EXCAVATOR

MAIN USE OF VEHICLE:
DIGGING DIFFERENT TYPES OF SOIL, DIGGING TRENCHES.

WHERE IT WAS FIRST MADE:
ENGLAND 1882.

FACT ABOUT VEHICLE:
EXCAVATORS CAN DO THE JOB OF UP TO 20 LABOURING PEOPLE.

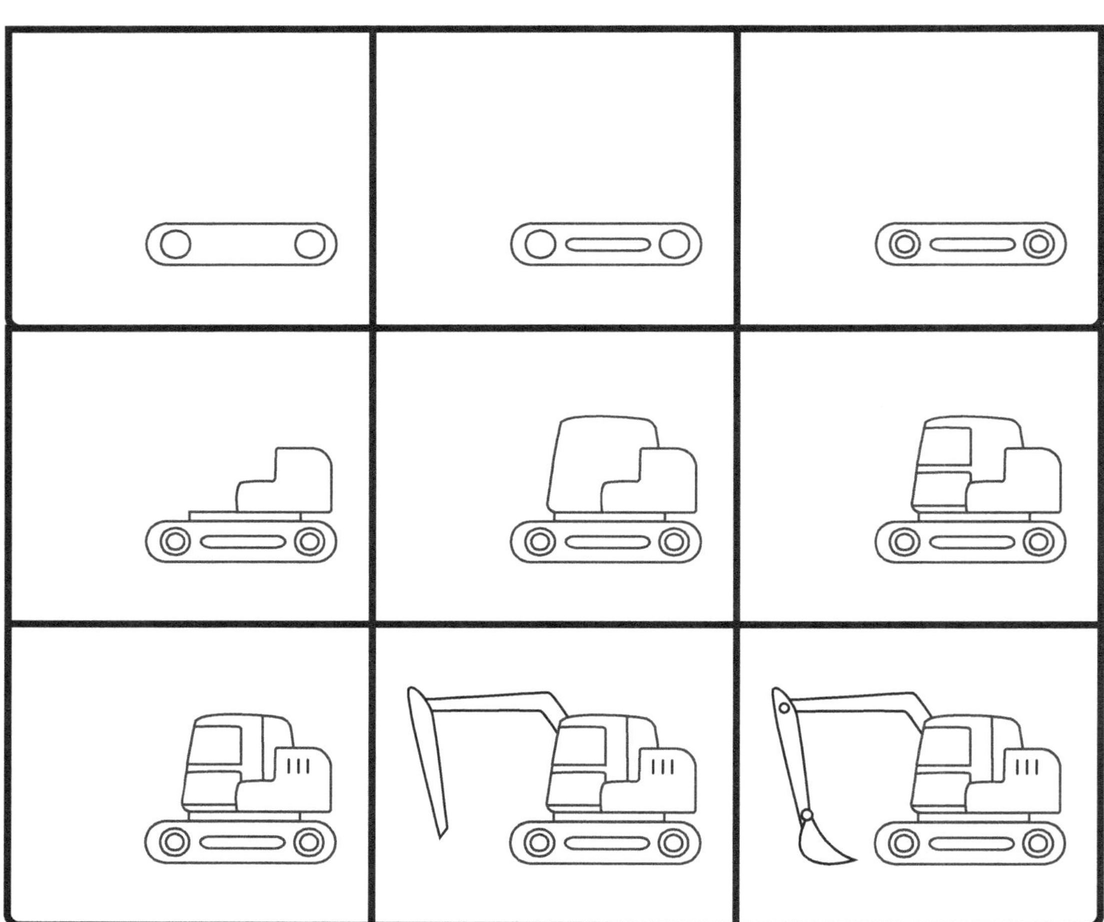

CONCRETE MIXER

MAIN USE OF VEHICLE:

USED AT BUILDING SITES TO MIX UP CONCRETE.

WHERE IT WAS FIRST MADE:

AMERICA 1900.

FACT ABOUT VEHICLE:

CONCRETE IS MADE FROM CEMENT, GRAVEL OR SAND, AND WATER.

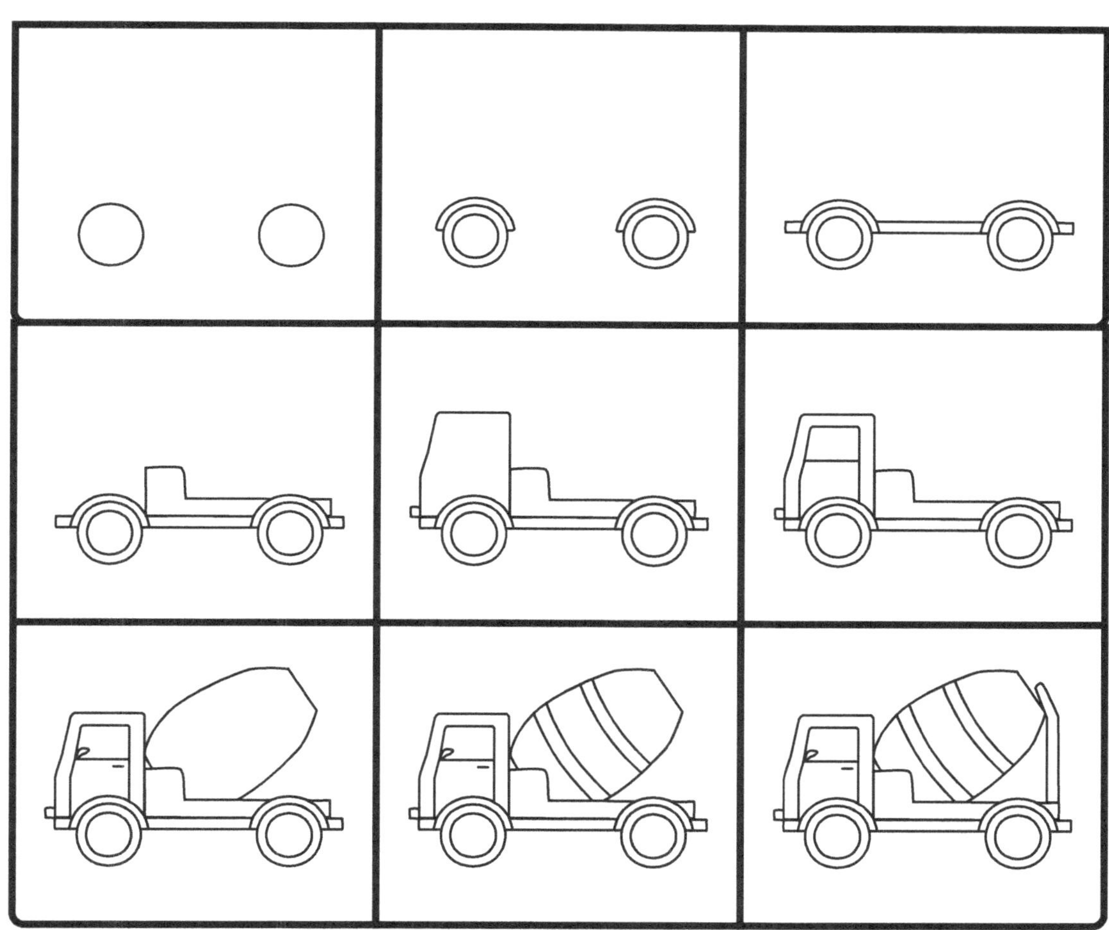

FRONT LOADER

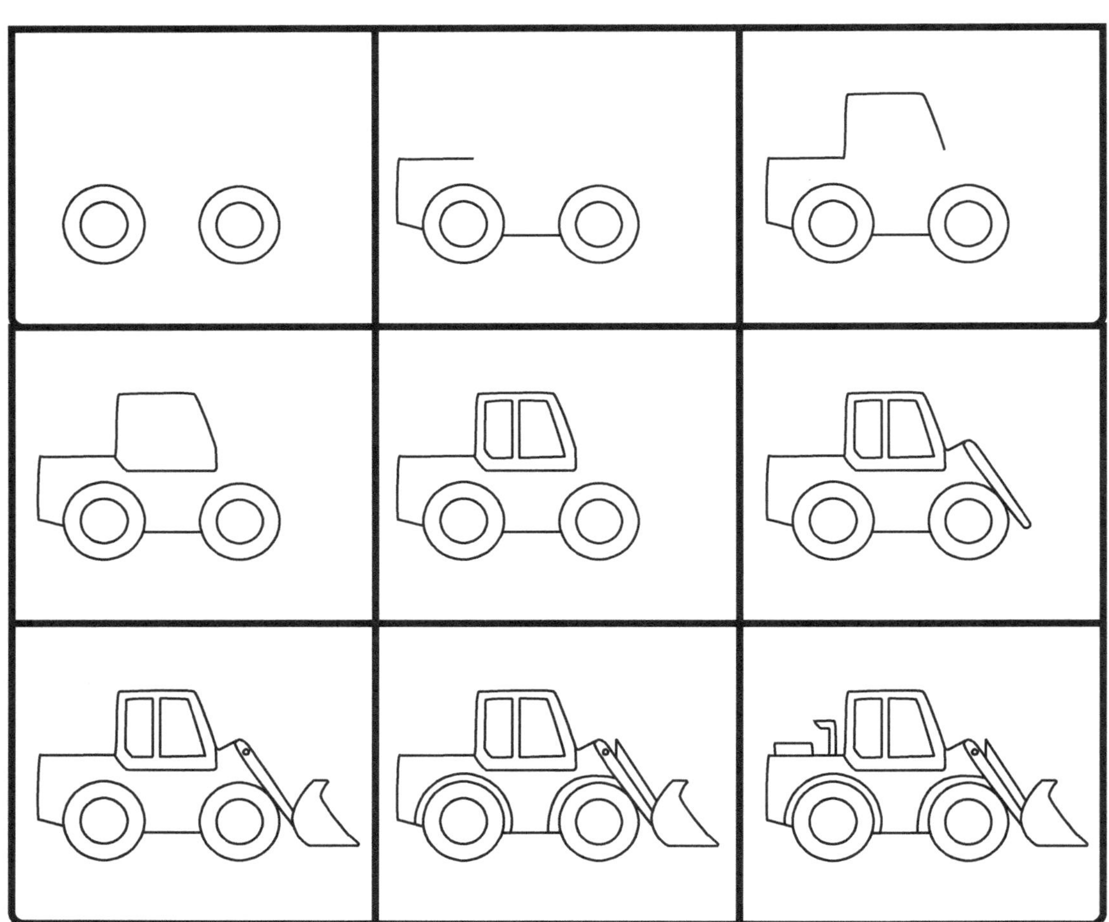

SKID STEER LOADER

TO DIG UP AND MOVE MATERIALS.

AMERICA 1957.

MANY PEOPLE CALL THEM BOBCATS, BUT THAT IS JUST A BRAND NAME.

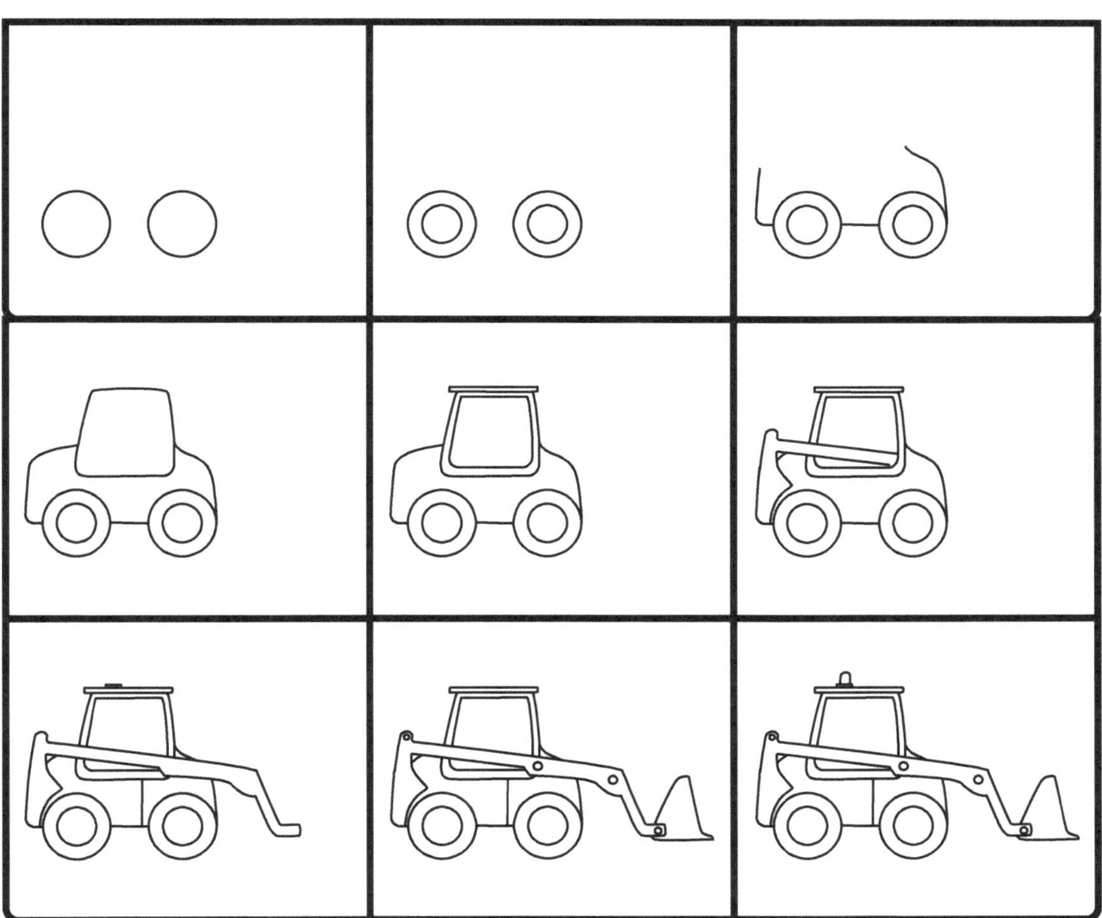

POLICE CAR

TO TRANSPORT POLICEMEN TO RESPOND TO THE NEEDS OF THE PEOPLE.

AMERICA 1899.

POLICE CAR DOORS ARE BULLETPROOF.

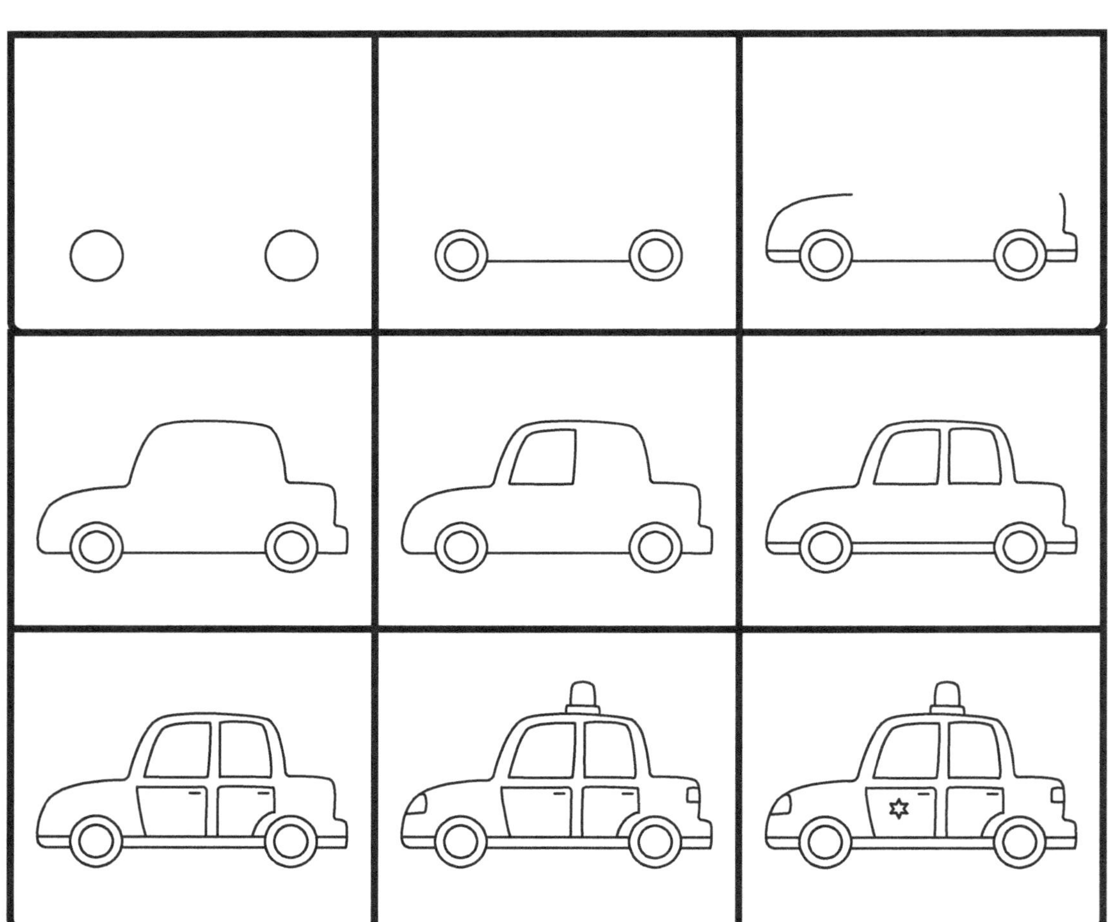

AMBULANCE

MAIN USE OF VEHICLE:
TO TRANSPORT SICK PEOPLE TO THE HOSPITAL AND GIVE EMERGENCY CARE.

WHERE IT WAS FIRST MADE:
AMERICA 1869.

FACT ABOUT VEHICLE:
HORSES AND WAGONS USED TO BE USED AS AMBULANCES.

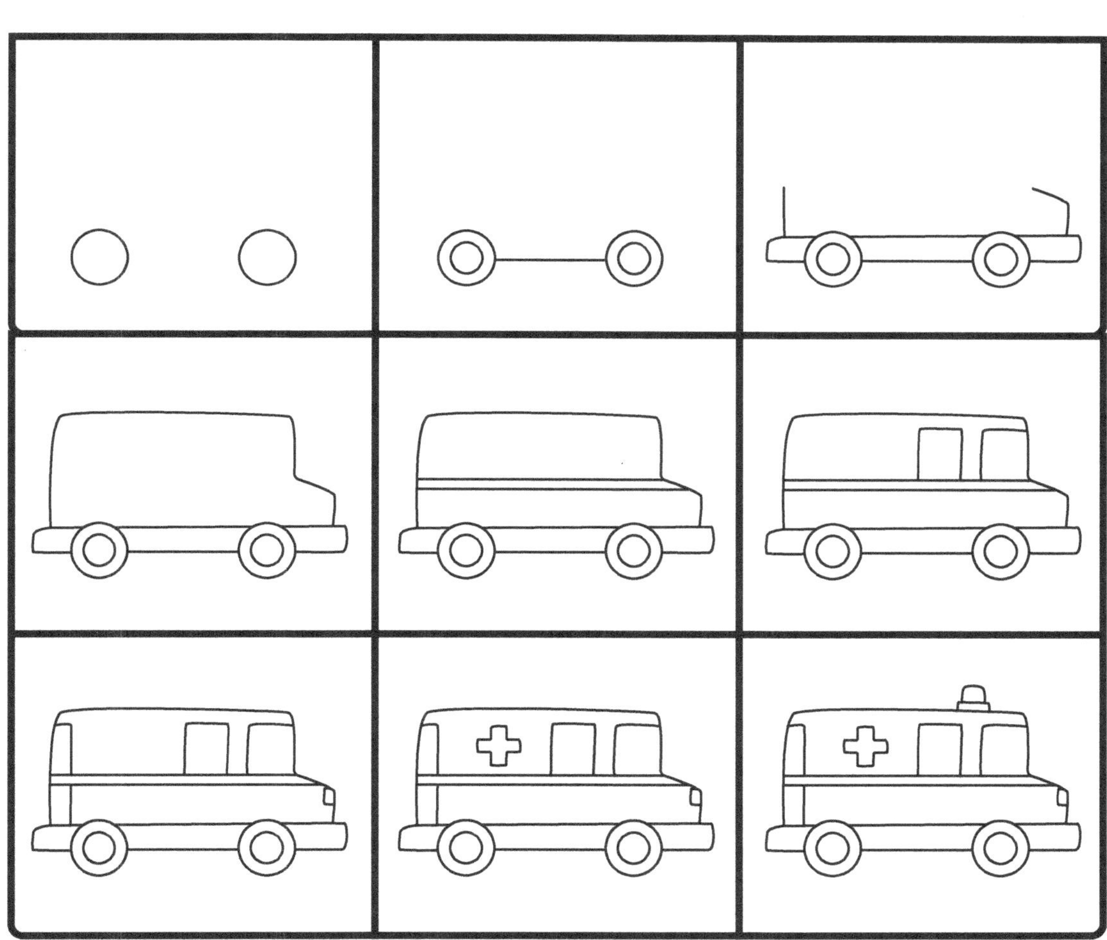

WHEELCHAIR

MAIN USE OF VEHICLE:

TO HELP MOVE PEOPLE ABOUT WHO HAVE DISABILITIES.

WHERE IT WAS FIRST MADE:

SPAIN 1595.

FACT ABOUT VEHICLE:

WHEELCHAIRS MAKE IT POSSIBLE FOR PEOPLE TO WORK, STUDY AND JOIN IN SPORTS, AND MORE.

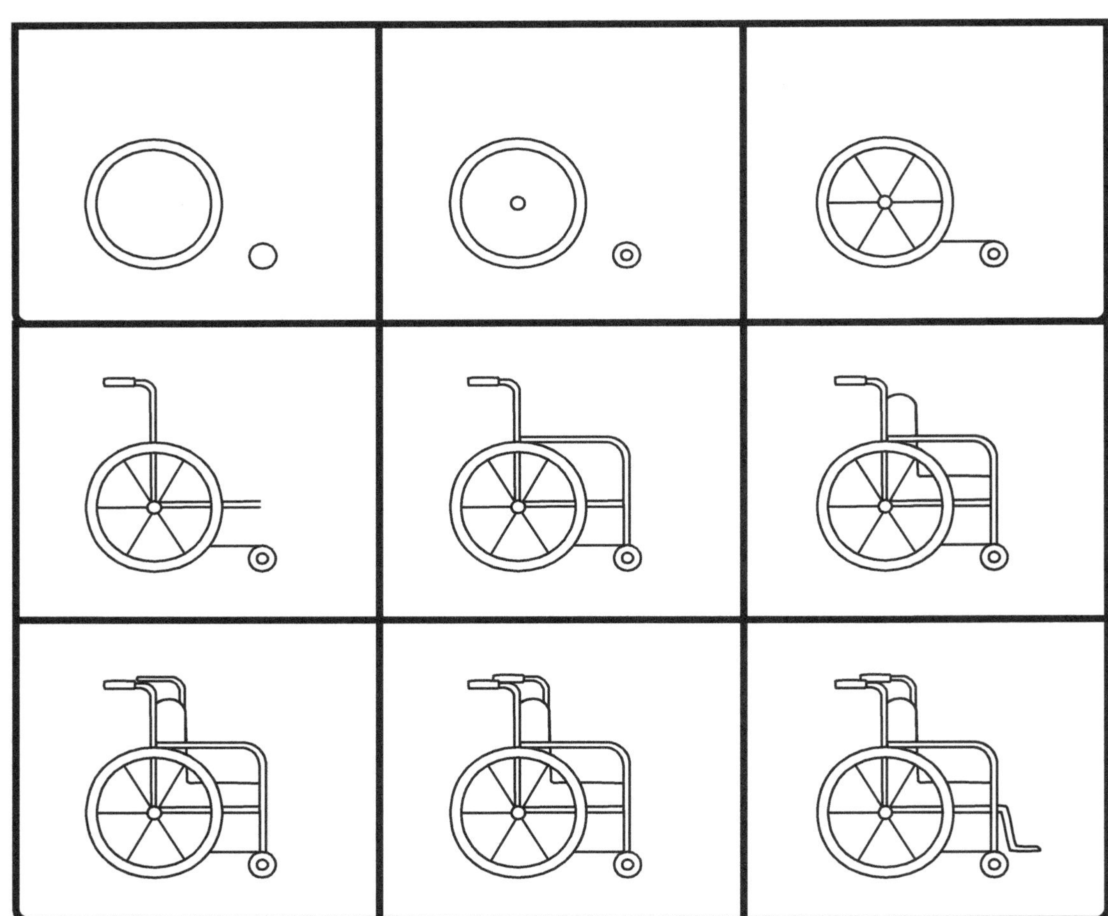

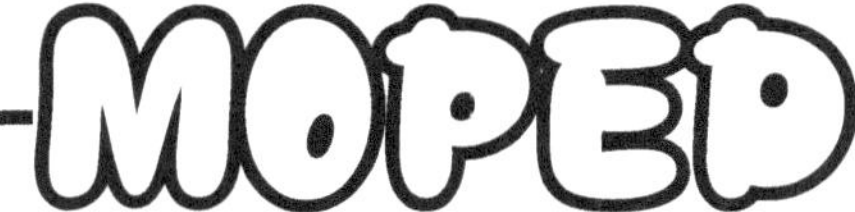

MOPED

MAIN USE OF VEHICLE:

GETTING PEOPLE ABOUT ON SHORT TRIPS.

WHERE IT WAS FIRST MADE:

AMERICA 1916.

FACT ABOUT VEHICLE:

THE WORD 'MOPED' COMES FROM JOINING THE WORDS, 'MOTOR' AND 'PEDAL'.

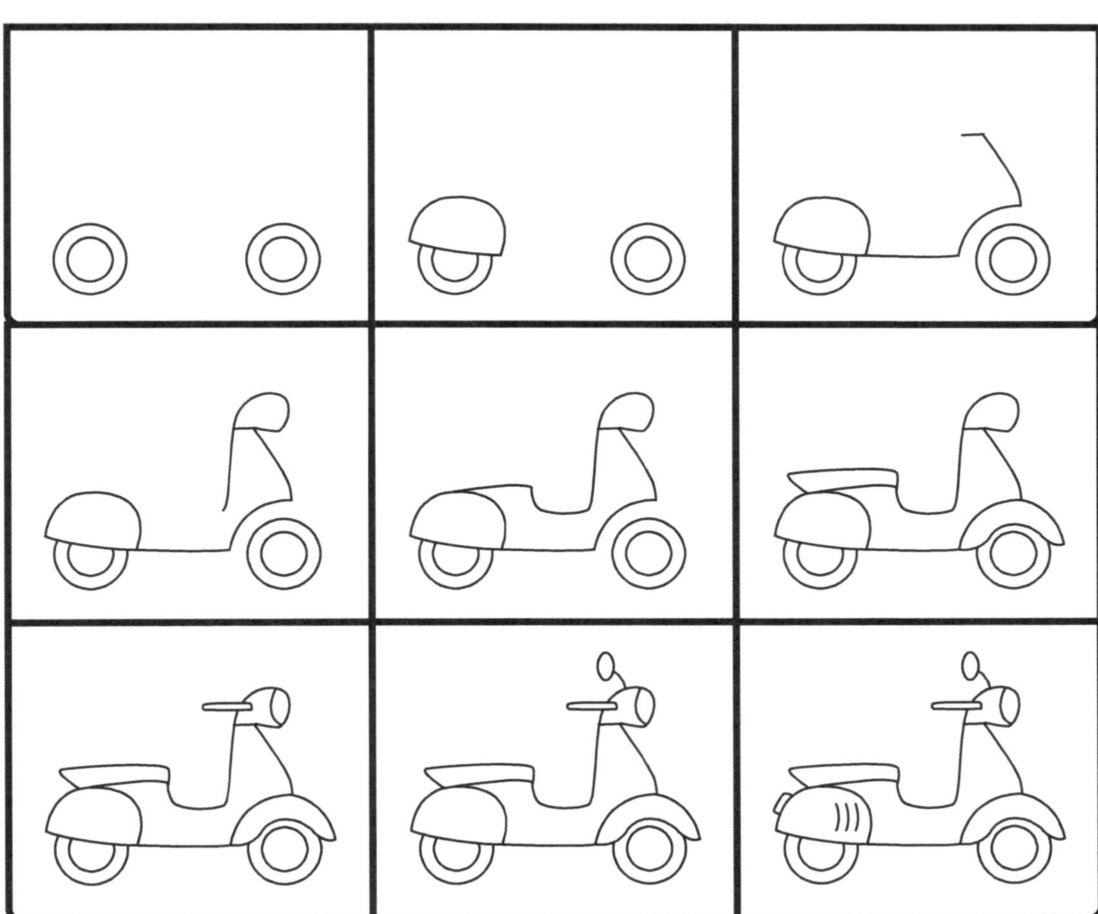

SNOWMOBILE

MAIN USE OF VEHICLE:
TO GET ABOUT AND HAVE FUN ON THE SNOW.

WHERE IT WAS FIRST MADE:
CANADA 1935.

FACT ABOUT VEHICLE:
THE AVERAGE SNOWMOBILER IS 45 YEARS OLD.

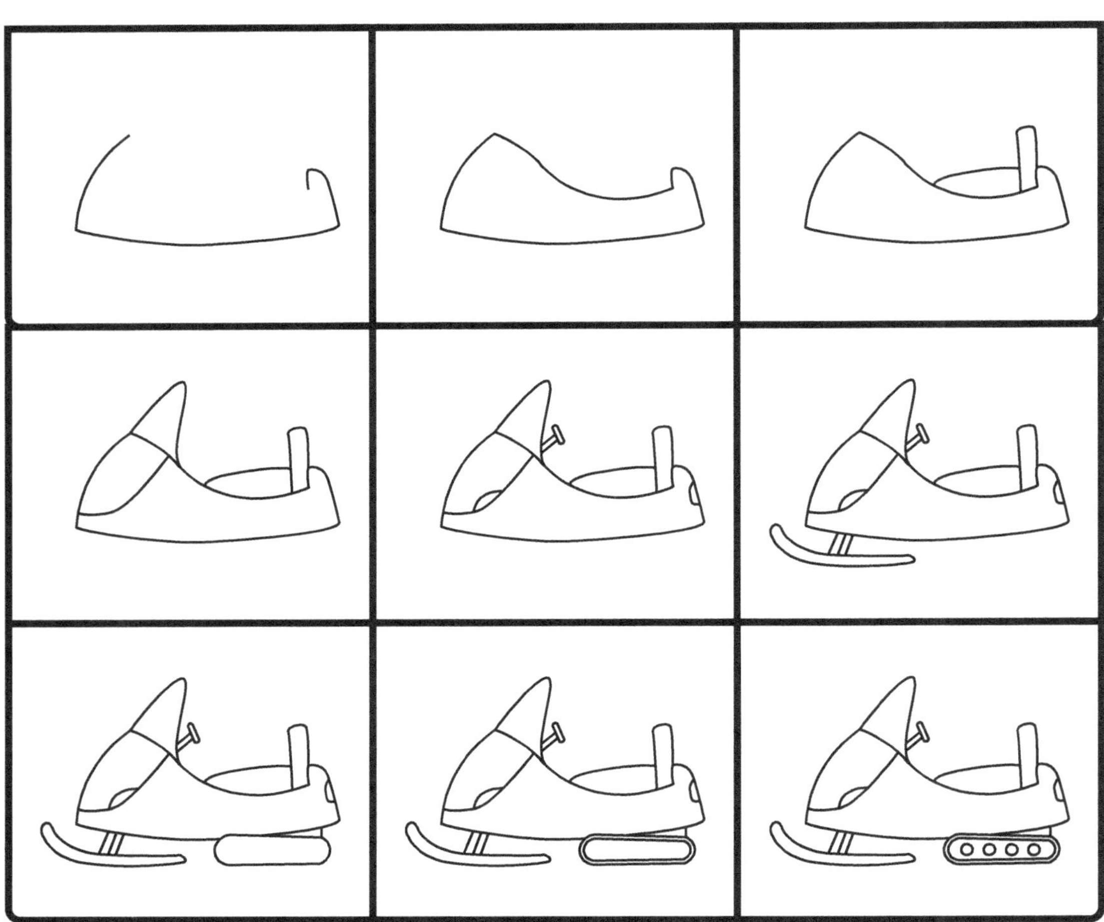

TRAM

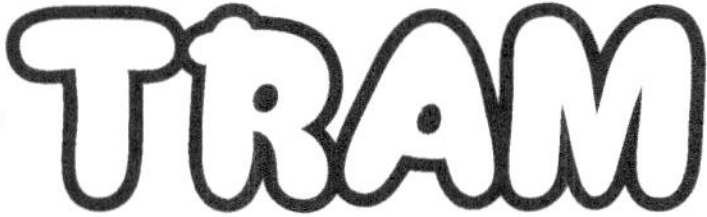

MAIN USE OF VEHICLE:
TO MOVE PEOPLE ABOUT IN CITIES.

WHERE IT WAS FIRST MADE:
RUSSIA 1875.

FACT ABOUT VEHICLE:
MORDEN TRAMS REPLACED HORSE-DRAWN TRAMS.

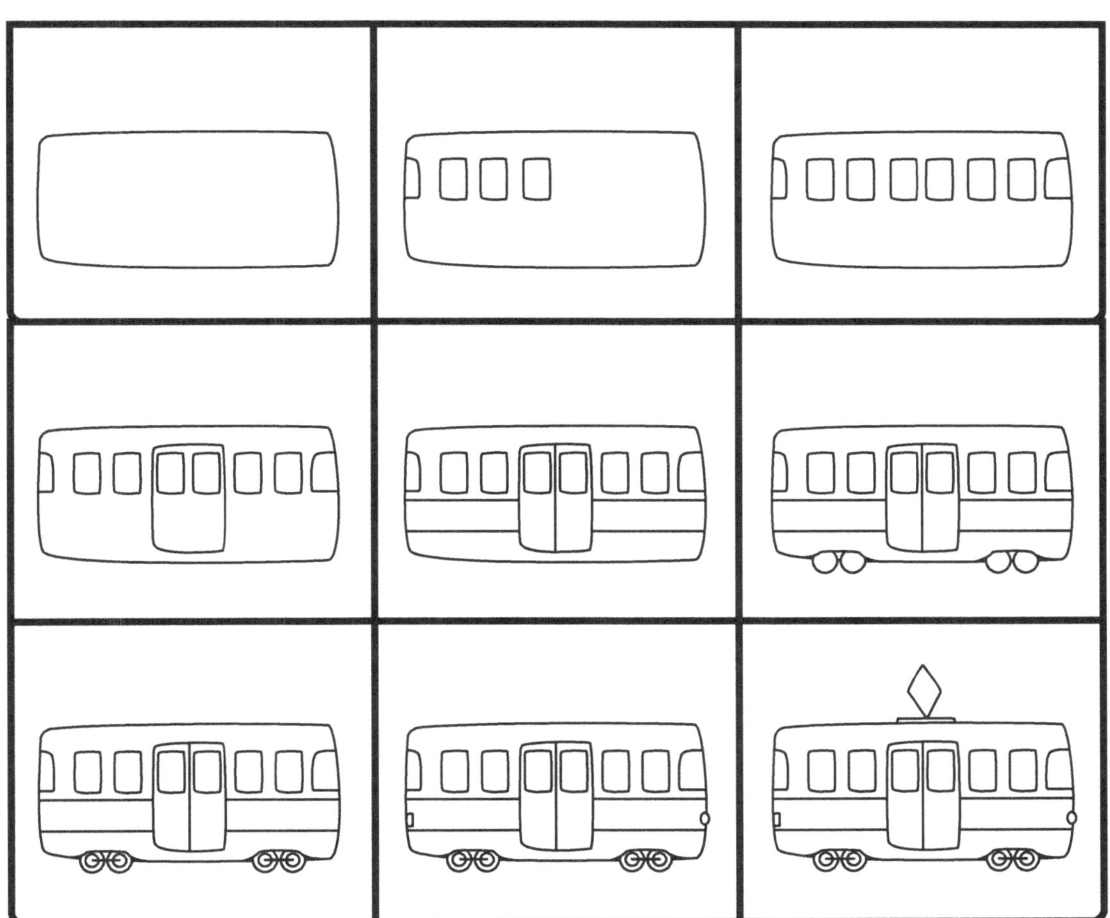

FORKLIFT

MAIN USE OF VEHICLE: TO LIFT AND MOVE HEAVY LOADS ABOUT.

WHERE IT WAS FIRST MADE: AMERICA 1917.

FACT ABOUT VEHICLE: FORKLIFTS ARE MAINLY USED IN FACTORIES AND WAREHOUSES.

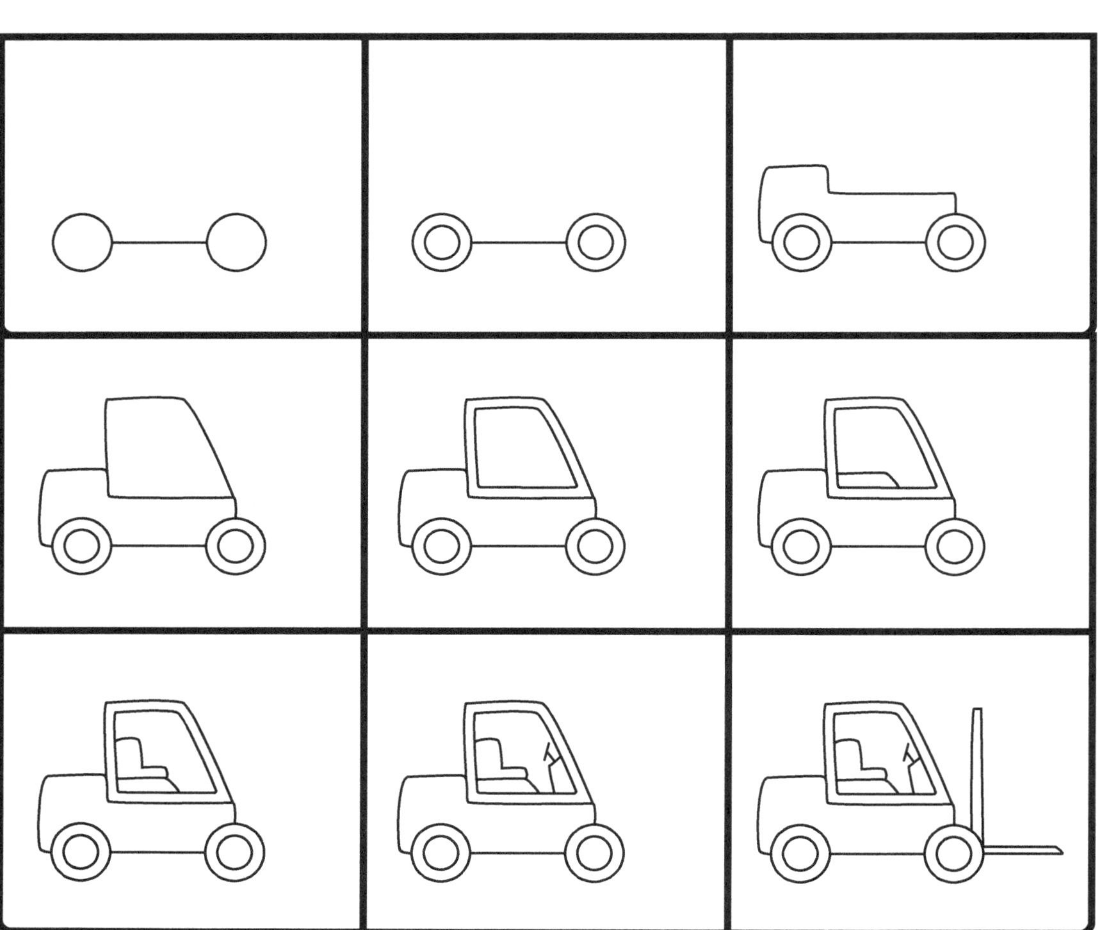

TAXI

MAIN USE OF VEHICLE:
TO TRANSPORT PEOPLE ABOUT.

WHERE IT WAS FIRST MADE:
GERMANY 1897.

FACT ABOUT VEHICLE:
PEOPLE JUST LOVE TALKING TO TAXI DRIVERS!

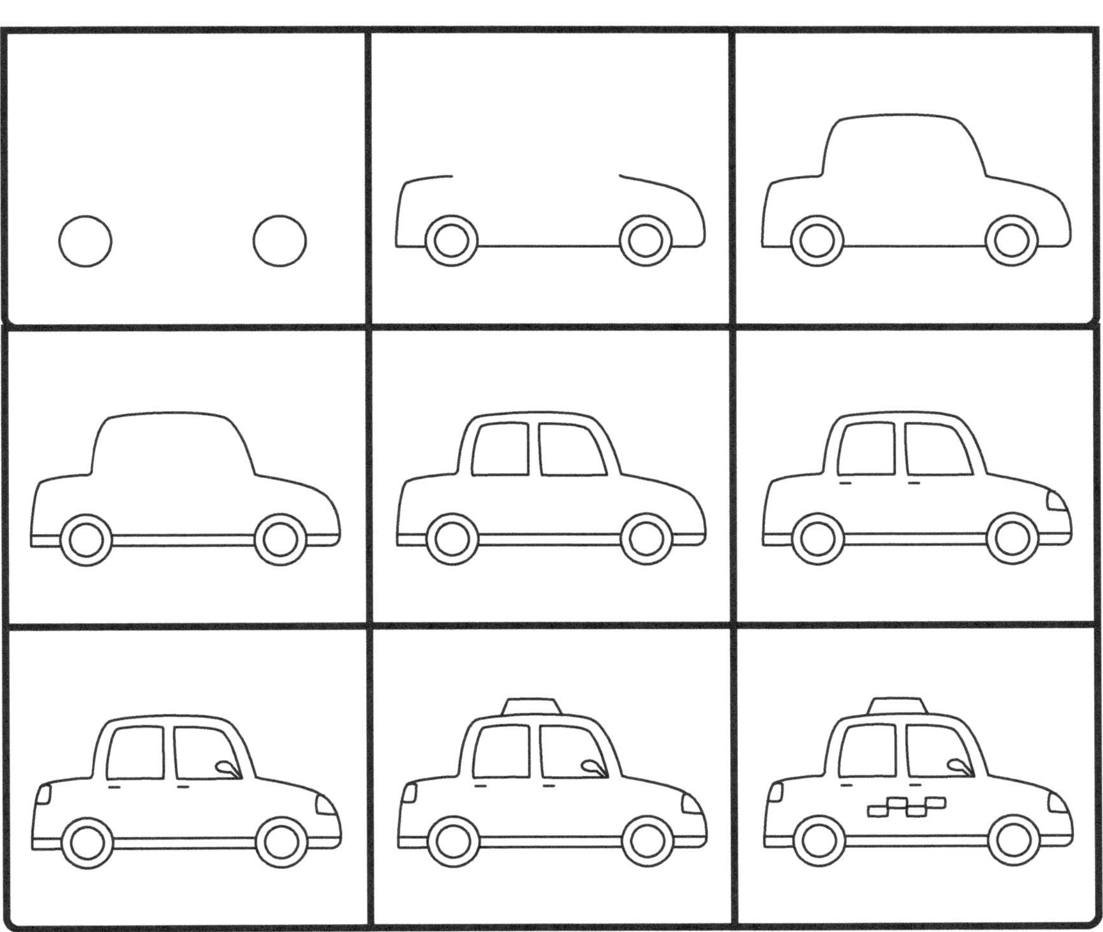

JEEP

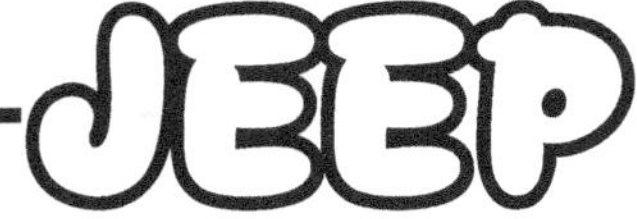

MAIN USE OF VEHICLE:
TO MOVE THE ARMY AND SUPPLIES ABOUT, RECREATION, AND SAFARI.

WHERE IT WAS FIRST MADE:
AMERICA 1940.

FACT ABOUT VEHICLE:
JEEPS DID NOT ALWAYS HAVE DOORS.

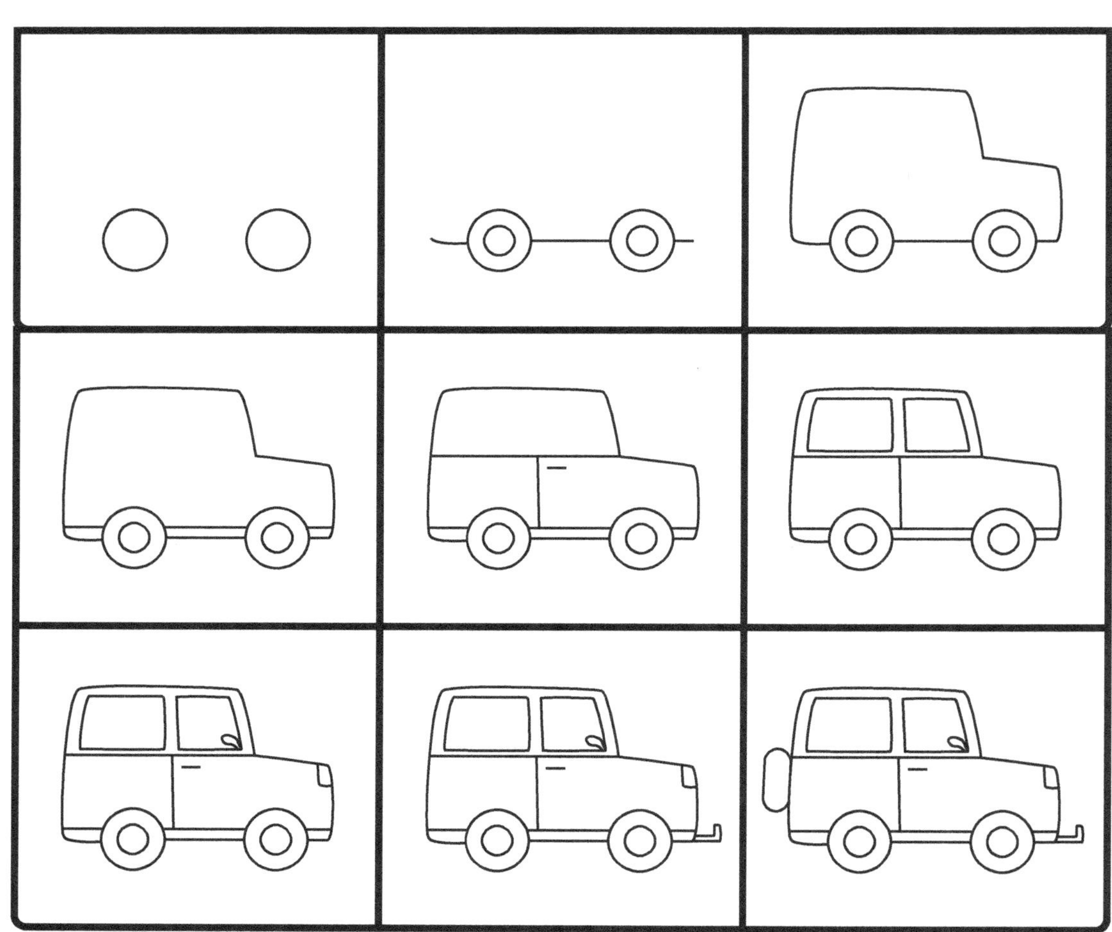

ANTIQUE CAR

MAIN USE OF VEHICLE:
RECREATION.

WHERE IT WAS FIRST MADE:
GERMANY 1888.

FACT ABOUT VEHICLE:
THEY ARE ALSO CALLED 'VINTAGE CARS.'

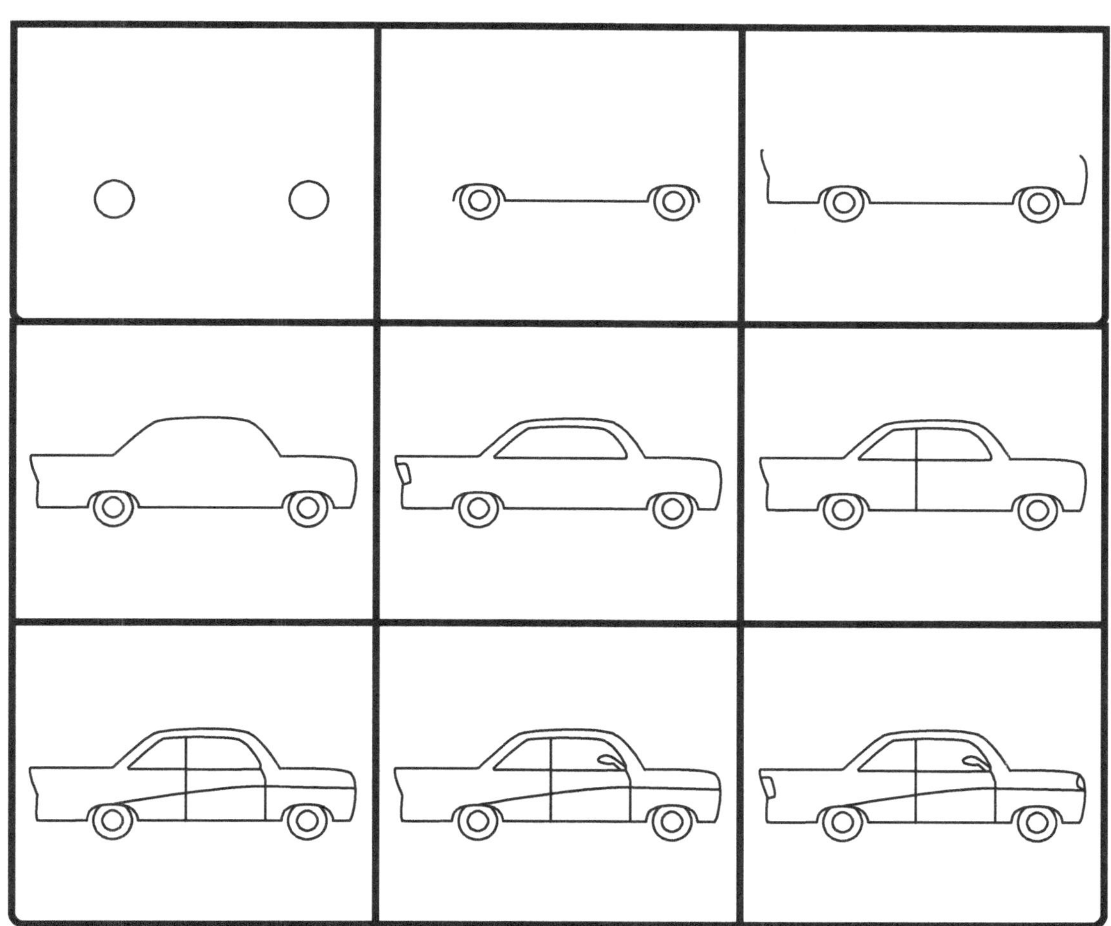

FUEL TRUCK

MAIN USE OF VEHICLE:
TO TRANSPORT LARGE AMOUNTS OF FUEL AND LIQUIDS.

WHERE IT WAS FIRST MADE:
AMERICA 1905.

FACT ABOUT VEHICLE:
THESE TRUCKS CAN BE USED AS MILK TRUCKS TOO.

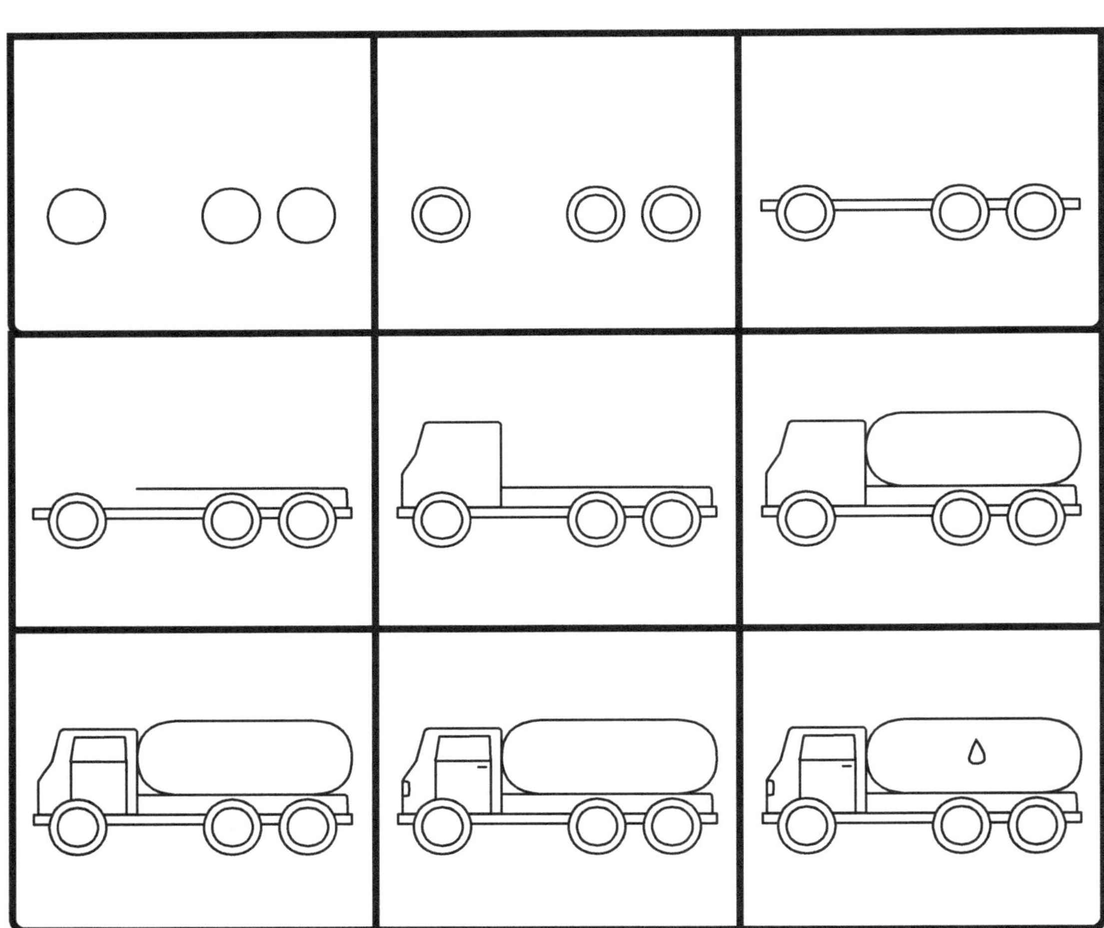

AIRSHIP

MAIN USE OF VEHICLE:
ADVERTISING, AND FILMING OF EVENTS.

WHERE IT WAS FIRST MADE:
FRANCE 1852.

FACT ABOUT VEHICLE:
THEY ARE ALSO CALLED BLIMPS.

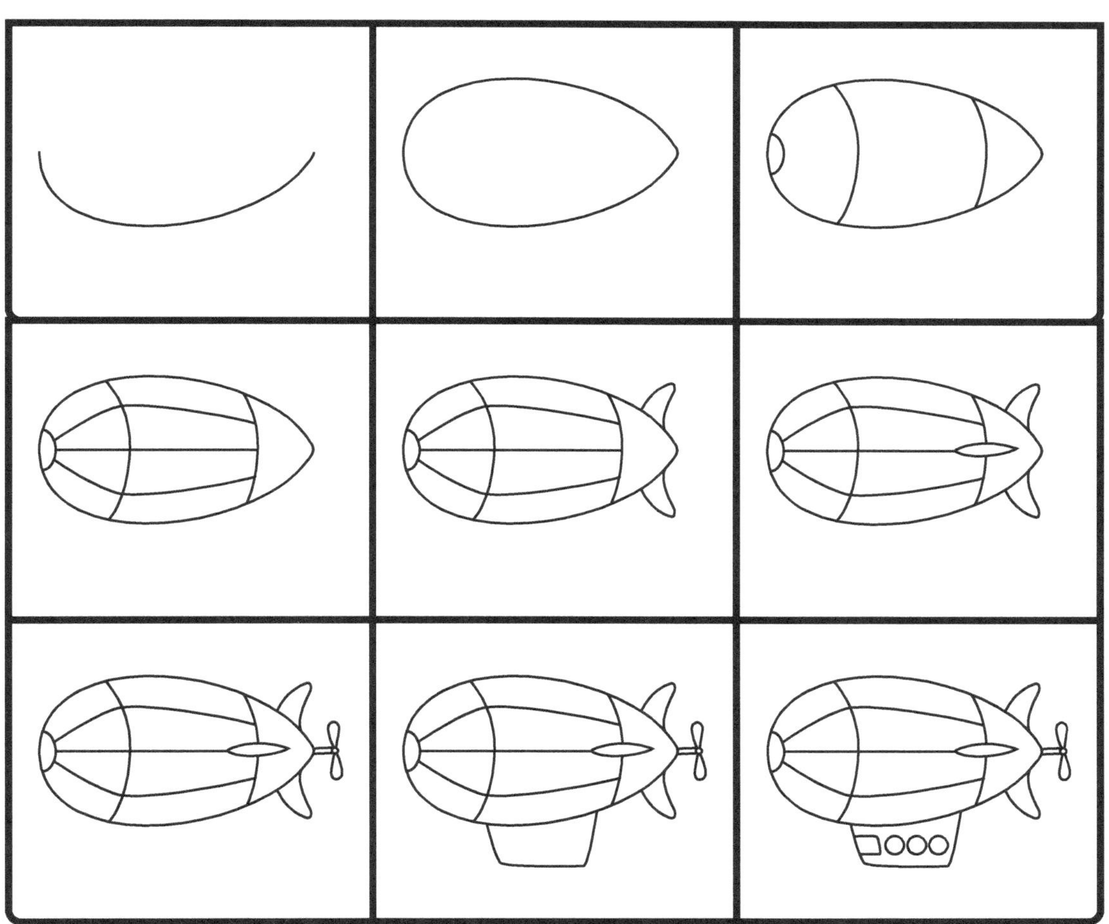

CARRIAGE

TO TRANSPORT PEOPLE AND GOODS DRIVEN BY HORSES.

MESOPOTAMIA 3000BC.

CARRIAGES WERE MOSTLY USED BY FANCY PEOPLE, LIKE ROYALS, AND WERE OFTEN BEAUTIFULLY DECORATED.

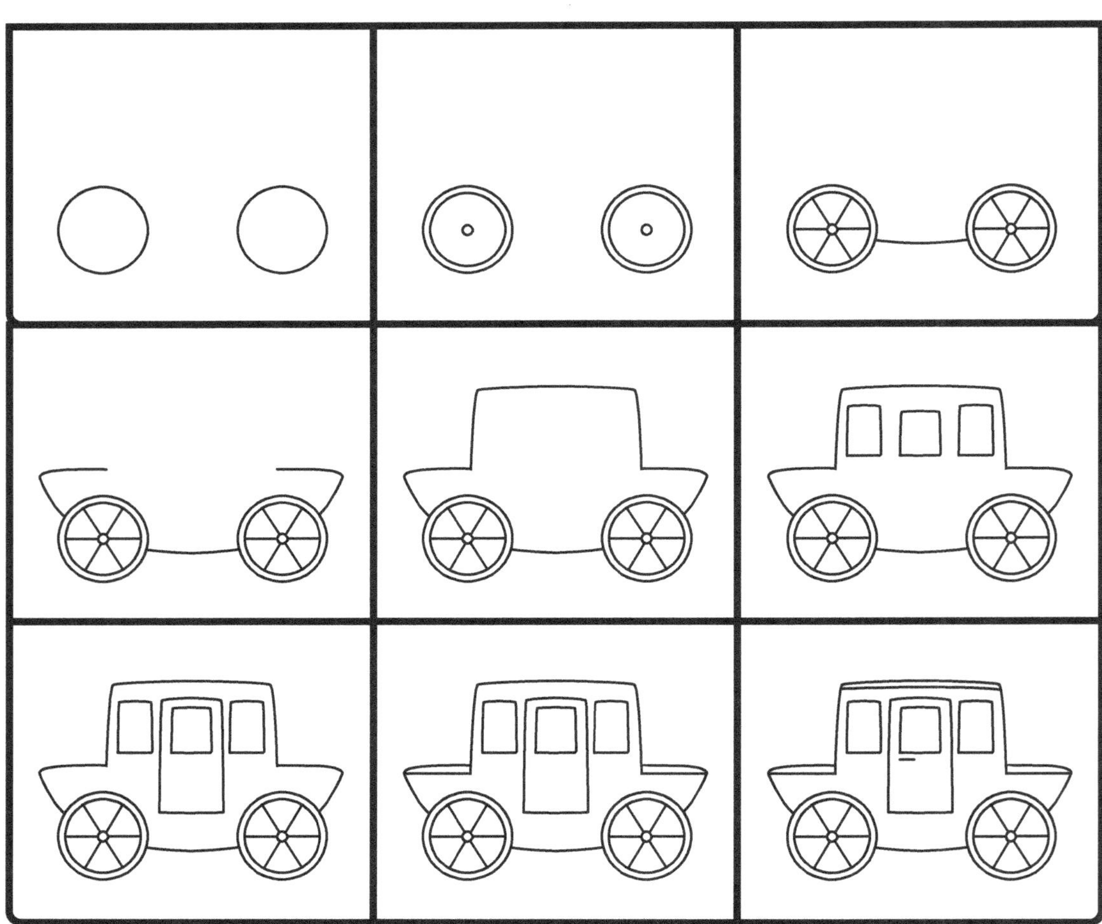

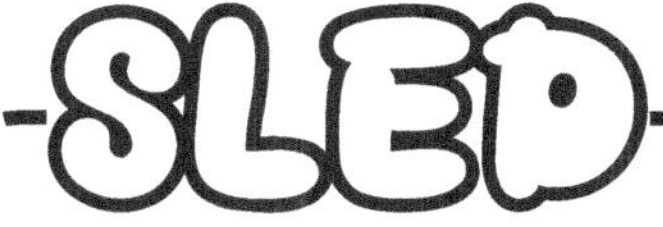

MAIN USE OF VEHICLE:

RECREATION AND TO CARRY GOODS AND PEOPLE ACROSS THE SNOW.

WHERE IT WAS FIRST MADE:

ANCIENT EGYPT.

FACT ABOUT VEHICLE:

THE WORD 'SLED' COMES FROM THE WORD 'SLEDDE' WHICH MEANS 'SLIDE' IN MIDDLE DUTCH.

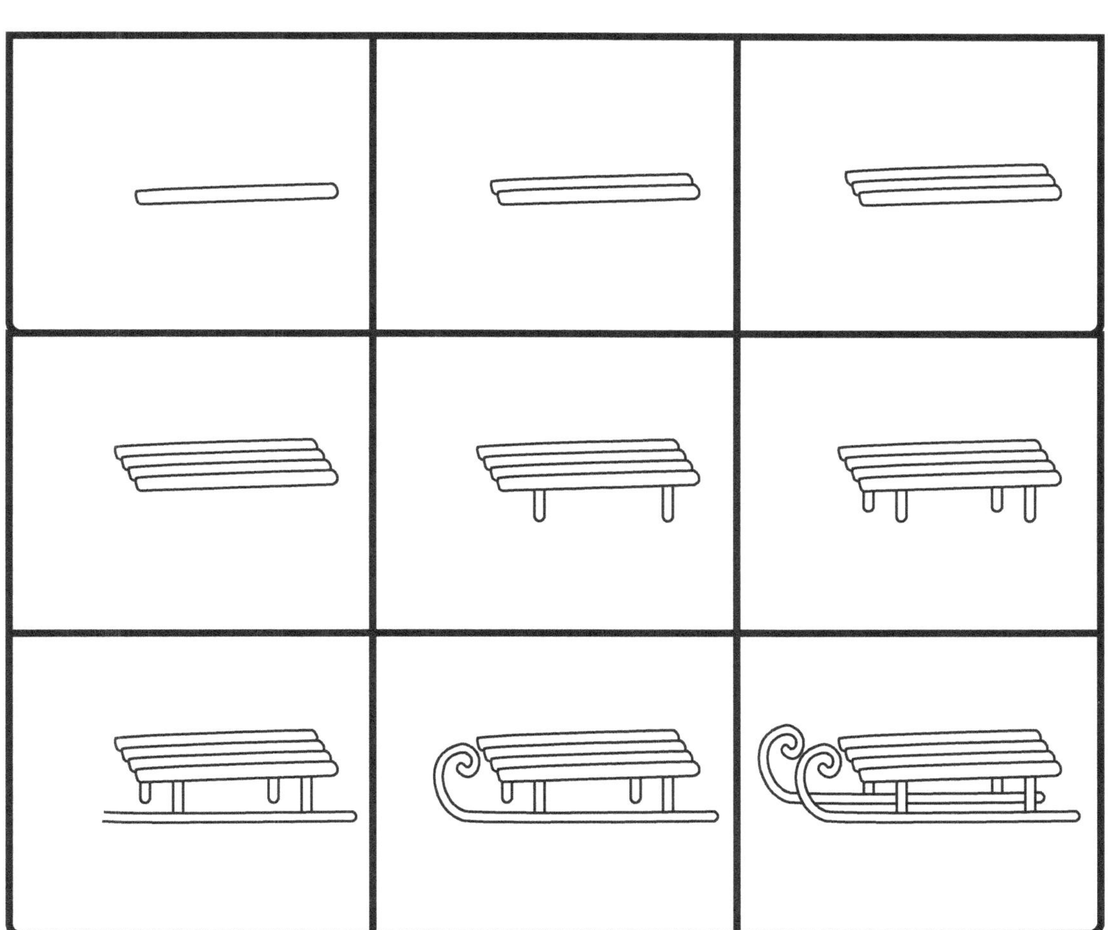

CONCLUSION

SO HOW DID YOU GO DRAWING THE VEHICLES? WERE SOME VEHICLES TRICKIER THAN OTHERS? OR SOME MORE FUN TO DRAW?

NOW THAT YOU KNOW THE BASICS OF DRAWING EACH VEHICLE, YOU CAN ADD YOUR OWN UNIQUE TOUCHES AND PERSONALITIES TO THEM!

IF YOU ENJOYED THE BOOK, PLEASE BE SURE TO LEAVE US A REVIEW ON AMAZON AS IT REALLY HELPS US GROW!

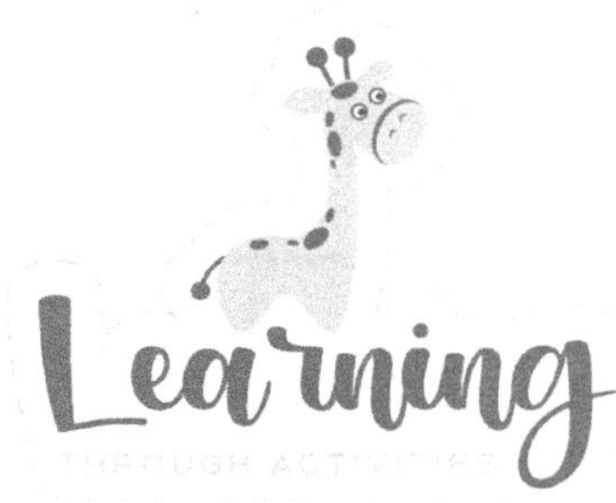